D1443511

THE ROAD TO THE CROSS

THE ROAD

TO THE CROSS

Herbert F. Stevenson

INTRODUCTION BY
PAUL S. REES

FLEMING H. REVELL COMPANY

Introduction

It just happens that this introductory word is being written in India. In the spacious mystical soul of this amazing land there is room for everything religious, indeed for everything Christian, save one: the uniqueness of Jesus Christ. When a representative of one of the more ethically refined Hindu sects asked a missionary what he meant by "salvation" and was given a simple, straightforward, Biblical reply, he remarked, "That is exactly what I would have said." "Oh," said the missionary, "what then is the ground of your assurance that God is ready to forgive you?" Unhesitatingly, he replied, "If He wouldn't, I would go to a God who would!"

The missionary made a point of the fact that this is typical of the "religious" approach to God, even at its best. It is not *supply*, but *need* of which one is supremely aware. For his yearning has no matching awareness that from the God-side the provision for the meeting of the need has been made. Therefore "God" to him is secondary: if one will not do, he will turn to another.

How immensely and gloriously otherwise is the Christian Gospel! The one living God of creation and judgment is likewise the God who has in fact, at a particular place and time in history, revealed His saving grace in behalf of the world of alien men.

The focus of that revelation is the cross and—indissolubly linked with it—the Resurrection.

What carries us *there* is good for us. What allures us away from *there* is ill for us.

It is the business of this book to plant our feet in the *Via Crucis*. Step by step the author leads us along. The lead he gives us is quiet and steady. It is not stormy, not peremptory. The feeling grows, however, that it is a competent hand by which we are being led.

Out here in India, years ago, the saintly and revered Bishop

5

Badley once composed a prayer, in which occur the moving lines—

> Christ, if ever my footsteps should falter,
>   And I be prepared for retreat,
> If desert or thorn cause lamenting,
>   Lord, show me Thy feet:
> Thy bleeding feet, Thy nail-scarred feet,
>   My Jesus, show me Thy feet.
>   *O God, dare I show Thee*
>   *My hands and my feet?*

Traveller, do take *the road to the cross*; and then you too will find this wistful prayer taking shape on your lips. Nor will the prayer be unaccompanied by the tremulous query—

> *O God, dare I show Thee*
> *My hands and my feet?*

PAUL S. REES

Foreword

This is not just another book about the Passion of our Lord. That theme is, indeed, the most sublime that the human mind can contemplate: yet the drama of Golgotha was but the focal point of a divine "plan of salvation" comprehending all eternity. For the crucifixion of Jesus of Nazareth was the fulfilment at a point in time of a divine purpose determined in the counsels of the Godhead before the creation of the world. To look upon the cross in relation to the entire sweep of that redeeming purpose, is to witness the ultimate expression of the supernal grace of God our Saviour. It is to witness the Son of the Most High identifying Himself with sinful men, in order to bear their guilt and accomplish their redemption. The corollary of that atoning activity is our identification—as His disciples—with the Lord Jesus, in His death and burial and resurrection. These wider aspects and implications are the subject of these meditations upon "the road to the cross"—and the glory that followed.

"Christ has been in agony from the foundation of the world."

BLAISE PASCAL

"To those who accept the Gospel histories, nothing is clearer than that the cross with its dark shadow lies upon them from the very beginning. The shadow of that cross is over His cradle, and even in the tranquil years of His childhood and youth it is not absent. An old legend describes Him as working out His own cross in the carpenter's shop at Nazareth. The Gospel is like one of those great tragedies where in the earlier scenes a suspicion is infused of the darkness that deepens round the close. The cross is always present from the very first, although more fully unveiled as time proceeds. The life of Jesus was a perpetual going forth to the cross."

W. ROBERTSON NICOLL

Contents

		Page
INTRODUCTION	. . . . . .	5
FOREWORD	. . . . .	7
1. ITS BEGINNING	. . . . . .	11
2. OLD TESTAMENT ANTICIPATIONS	. . .	15
3. FROM THE THRONE TO THE MANGER	. .	19
4. FIRST SIGHT OF THE CITY	. . . .	23
5. NUMBERED WITH THE TRANSGRESSORS	. .	29
6. FACE TO FACE WITH THE DEVIL	. . .	33
7. COMPANIONS FOR THE WAY	. . . .	40
8. DECISIVE CROSS-ROADS	. . . .	45
9. CLASH WITH AUTHORITY	. . . .	52
10. PERILS OF POPULARITY	. . . .	59
11. VIEWED FROM A MOUNTAIN	. . .	65
12. A PAUSE AT BETHANY	. . . .	71
13. THE KING COMES TO HIS CITY	. . .	79
14. OLIVET'S FOREGLIMPSE OF THE FUTURE	. .	85
15. A MEAL WITH THE TWELVE	. . .	91
16. PRAYER IN A GARDEN	. . . .	98
17. JEWISH AND GENTILE JUDGES	. . .	105
18. ARRIVAL AT GOLGOTHA	. . . .	112
19. AND THE GLORY THAT FOLLOWED	. .	119
20. OUR IDENTIFICATION WITH CHRIST	. .	124

Alone Thou goest forth, O Lord,
   In sacrifice to die;
Is this Thy sorrow naught to us
   Who pass unheeding by?

Our sins, not Thine, Thou bearest, Lord;
   Make us Thy sorrow feel,
Till through our pity and our shame
   Love answers love's appeal.

This is earth's darkest hour, but Thou
   Canst light and life restore;
Then let all praise be given to Thee
   Who livest evermore.

Grant us to suffer with Thee, Lord,
   That, as we share this hour,
Thy cross may bring us to Thy joy
   And resurrection power.

PETER ABELARD

1

Its Beginning

CRUCIFIXION was the most terrible form of the death-penalty which Imperial Rome could devise. It was the supreme torture which an iron-shod despotism could impose upon subject peoples who dared to withstand its authority or violate its laws. At the threat of it, men who feared nothing else would blench; and among the privileged citizens of Rome it was regarded as too abhorrent even to be contemplated. "May the very name of a cross be far removed, not only from the bodies of Roman citizens," said Cicero, "but even from their thoughts, their sight, their hearing."

The cross was, on the one hand, the symbol of Rome's stern domination; and on the other, of the ultimate degradation to which a human being could be condemned. From it, as from nothing else, all men would shrink in loathing and fear. Yet there was One who chose a course which He knew would lead to a cross: who steadfastly set His face toward that culmination and climax of His life, with unflinching, unfaltering determination. "For this cause," He declared, as He stood under the very shadow of the cross, "came I unto this hour."

From early times in Church history, it has been the custom of Christian people to contemplate *Via Crucis*—the road to the cross—and especially during the forty days preceding Good Friday, as a preparation of heart and mind for a worthy remembrance of the Passion of our Lord. Nonconformity, however, recoiled from the observance of Lent, as of other "times and seasons," in avoidance of everything even remotely savouring of Romanism. It is significant, however, that in recent years the Free Churches are increasingly realising the value of sustained meditation, in the weeks before Good Friday and Eastertide, upon the events of the last days of the life of our Lord. Apart from the personal benefit to individuals, in thus contemplating the cross, there is surely a "fellowship of saints" of inestimable value, as the Church of Christ—made up of members of many denominations—think and pray day by day upon the same foundational verities in which all are united.

The road to the cross had its beginning, of course, not at Cæsarea Philippi—where, for convenience, Lenten meditations customarily commence; nor at the baptism of Jesus in Jordan, where He was "numbered with the transgressors"; nor even at His birth in Bethlehem. Looking farther back to the Garden, where our first parents sinned: not even there had this road its beginnings. Peter tells us that our Lord was "foreordained before the foundation of the world" to be the Redeemer of mankind (1 Peter 1: 20). It was in the eternal counsels of God that this road had its origin. St. John also acclaims our Lord Jesus as "the Lamb slain from the foundation of the world" (Rev. 13: 8).

The cross, then, was not a rescue-operation devised to modify the disastrous effects of the Fall. Adam's transgression did not take God by surprise, and necessitate a desperate counter-measure, which involved God in such a hazardous venture as the sending of His Son to lead some of the dupes of Satan into a renewal of loyalty to God. That thought seems to underlie the attitude of some folk toward the Gospel.

But creation was not an experiment. God did not take a tremendous risk, earnestly hoping that the creature made in His image and likeness, and gifted with freewill, would choose to love and obey Him, rather than respond to the seductions of the tempter. God did not watch with breathless wonder and excitement the drama of the Garden: He knew before He created Adam how he would use his free-will, and all the evil consequences that would follow. Together with the determination to create man, however, was the fore-ordination of Christ as the Lamb of God: in our human likeness to redeem a fallen race, and to reconcile man to God in a fellowship of responding love which should satisfy and rejoice His heart eternally.

Herein lies a mystery not easily explained. There is no facile answer to the deep problems of divine sovereignty and human sinfulness. To enter, even in limited measure, into an understanding of the mind and ways of God concerning man's creation and redemption, we must carefully compare Scripture with Scripture, and be ready to learn humbly, line upon line. In such a study of the Word we apprehend that God, worshipped and adored as He was by the heavenly host, could be satisfied—in His desire for true *fellowship*—only in the love and willing obedience of beings created in His own image and likeness. A homage which would eternally rejoice His heart, must be rendered of free choice and volition; of deliberate will and intent.

To give the man He fashioned out of the earth such powers of choice to love and serve Him, meant also the endowment of free-will to choose otherwise: it involved the capacity to rebel and to sin. And God knew not only Adam's potentiality of sinning, but foreknew that he *would* sin. And so in heaven was devised—if one may reverently use that term of the eternal counsels of the Godhead—the "plan of redemption" whereby He would triumph over all the wiles of Satan in effecting Adam's fall, and would achieve His purpose despite the ravages and sad consequences of sin, in the estrangement of fallen man from Him.

More than that: not only would the effects of sin and death be nullified, and man restored to communion with his Creator, but through the very experience of temptation and sin and redemption His people would be brought into a relationship and condition which they could never have known by creative fiat. For the redeemed in Christ become *sons of God*; they are born into His family, and made heirs of God, joint-heirs with Christ; members of His Body; corporately, His Bride—

> . . . in Him the sons of Adam boast
> More blessings than their father lost.

In the Garden, Satan sought to rob God of His delight in man; to frustrate His purpose in creating the human race. Yet, with the strange short-sightedness repeatedly manifest in the devices of the devil, in so doing he *wrought the very purpose of God*. For sinners redeemed render Him a love and devotion which unfallen beings can never know. "Man falling," one has well said, "fell into the arms of the divine mercy."

That greater, over-riding purpose of God; that supreme manifestation of His mercy, entailed the cross. There was no

13

other way by which the devil's seeming triumph could be cancelled out, and overwhelmed by the greater triumph of the Lord. God could not forgive sin by a word; no decree even from the throne on high could pardon it, consistently with His character as the high and holy One. There was one way only for man's restoration: the bearing of his guilt and the blotting out of his sin by a substitute able to satisfy the demands of God's outraged Law, and to bestow newness of life, so that the guilty sinner might be born anew—might become a new creation.

Only One could be such a sin-bearer; for He must needs be holy, harmless, undefiled, separate from sinners; guileless and spotless, a Lamb without blemish: and so Jesus was ordained in eternal ages, the Lamb slain from the foundation of the world. And through His atoning death, with its triumph over sin and Satan, He is the Prince and Author of life; the Giver of eternal life to all who trust Him. By His Atonement He achieved the cherished purpose of God.

Unto that goal He must needs tread the way of the cross . . . not only in His humiliation, but from the very beginnings of the divine purposes in the creation of man, before the world was. He loved us with an everlasting love—reaching back to eternal ages past, as well as unto all future eternity: and in the fulfilling of that purpose of love He never deviated nor faltered.

2

Old Testament Anticipations

ALTHOUGH the beginning of the road to the cross reaches back beyond the limits of our finite horizons, we can clearly trace its course from the very dawn of human history. As we seek to tread it, however, in fellowship with the One who walked it steadfastly for us men and our salvation, we must remember that we are on holy ground.

The involvement of the eternal Son of God in our human lot, as the Lamb slain from the foundation of the world, is a mystery surpassing our grasp of thought: we know it is wondrously true, and we enjoy its benefits; but it is one of the great verities of our Faith which are spiritually discerned, rather than intellectually apprehended. As the heavens are higher than the earth, so are His ways higher than our ways, and His thoughts than ours.

This is essentially true concerning His Person, and His preincarnate experience. There are glimpses afforded us in various Scriptures which enable us to understand in part: but we must beware of going beyond the explicit revelation of the Word. We have the warrant of our risen Lord, however, for discerning "in all the Scriptures the things concerning Himself" —and that, "beginning at Moses and all the prophets" (Luke 24: 27).

Now Paul is insistent that, in His Passion, Jesus suffered for sin *once for all* (Rom. 6: 10); and this is reaffirmed by the writer of the Epistle to the Hebrews (7: 27; 9: 26–28), and by Peter in his first Epistle (3: 18). This is a key-stone of Reformation doctrine; and it repudiates the Romanist teaching of repeated sacrifice upon the altar at Mass. Yet, holding this truth tenaciously, as we do, we nevertheless recognise a continuing of travail on the part of our ascended Lord, in and through the sins of His people. The writer to the Hebrews speaks of

15

those who, lapsing into sin, "crucify to themselves the Son of God afresh." Now we know this is anthropomorphic language: the bringing of the things of God into the realm of our experience and understanding. But while we recognise that our great High Priest is enthroned in triumph, His redeeming work accomplished, nevertheless He is not aloof and remote from our sin and suffering and sorrows.

> Where high the heavenly temple stands,
> The house of God not made with hands,
> A great high priest our nature wears,
> The guardian of mankind appears . . .
>
> Though now ascended up on high,
> He bends on earth a brother's eye;
> Partaker of the human name,
> He knows the frailty of our frame.
>
> Our fellow-suff'rer yet retains
> A fellow-feeling of our pains;
> And still remembers in the skies
> His tears, His agonies, and cries.
>
> In ev'ry pang that rends the heart,
> The Man of sorrows had a part;
> He sympathises with our grief,
> And to the sufferer sends relief . . .

This is the paraphrase of Hebrews 4: 14–16 in the Scottish *Psalter in Metre*, and it expresses most graphically our glorified Lord's present participation in our human distresses. He is the Man in the midst of the throne. The one Mediator between God and men is the Man Christ Jesus. And identified with us, as Head of His Body, Federal Head of the new creation, He enters into our human needs and vicissitudes. That is one of the most precious realities of our faith.

Can we say, then, that He does not *suffer* when His people sin; that there is not a continuing entail of the cross? Paul aspired to "know Him, and the fellowship of His sufferings, being made conformable unto His death." If there is for us, His people, a fellowship with the Lord in identification with Him in His death and burial and resurrection, then that fellowship of His cross is not merely an experience of ours: it is one we enter into in fellowship *with Him*. It is a present experience, not merely an assent to an event enacted in the past; and He has His part in it, as we have ours.

In this dispensation of grace, we—His people—are identified with the Lord Jesus in His cross; in the Old Testament era, He was identified with a sinful race as the Lamb slain from the foundation of the world. The benefits of His atoning death on Calvary reached back to the sin of Adam, just as they avail for all mankind in this dispensation of grace, until the moment of His Return in glory. Likewise, as He is intimately concerned in our sin and its consequences, so was He from the first sin of the first man in the Garden. We cannot conceive Him aloof, remote from sinners in olden times, any more than He is from us: viewing events impassively from the lofty heights of His throne. His identification with man, as sin-bearer and Saviour, entailed His walking the road to the cross from the very tree of the knowledge of good and evil, in Eden.

Adam was fashioned by the hands of the pre-incarnate Lord: for "by Him were all things created" (Col. 1 : 16). Can we not imagine His joy in this being, made in His image and likeness? Albeit He knew that that pristine splendour would soon be tarnished and the image defaced, yet God looked upon His handiwork and saw that it was good. And can we not imagine His anguish when Adam sinned, although He foreknew what would happen? Within our limited human experience, we know that our children will err, and can often anticipate specific misdeeds: but that fact does not mitigate our sorrow when they do commit them. His was the travail of the Creator-Redeemer: and in the slaying of a sacrifice to provide for fallen man a covering, He experienced in time the first stab of the sword which brought forth from His side blood mingled with water.

Adam's sin, and the attendant establishment of propitiatory sacrifice, presaged, from the Garden of Eden, the provision to be made by the one truly effectual offering for sin for ever. And the unfolding drama of the sad consequences of the fall, involved the predestined Redeemer ever more deeply in the very life and destiny of the race. Thus when Cain slew Abel he not only lifted up his hand against his brother, but he smote also the One who would take the totality of human sin upon His own pure soul, in order to destroy it in death upon the cross. Already He was treading the road which led to Calvary.

In every offering presented upon an altar of the patriarchs, His one sacrifice for sin for ever was, not merely portrayed, but prophetically enacted. The cross was ever before Him. Every sacrifice was, for the Lamb of God, a step along the road that led inevitably to Golgotha. The efficacy of the death of the cross was imparted to every sacrifice offered in true repentance and humble faith: not merely by a transaction of heavenly book-keeping, surely, but by a spiritual identification on the part of our Lord with sinners and their sin-offering.

Thus He proceeded along the road, its milestones provided by the rugged altars of the patriarchs, by the calling of a nation out of Egypt, by the giving of the Law and institution of the ritual of tabernacle and temple.

"Beginning at Moses and all the prophets . . ." Among those prophets, Isaiah especially foresaw the day of His humiliation. First, however, he "saw the Lord, high and lifted up; and His train filled the temple." This vision, John explicitly tells us, was of the pre-incarnate Lord Jesus (John 12: 41). Then the prophet, with lips cleansed by the touch of a live coal from off the altar—the altar which pre-figured the cross—told of a Suffering Servant, who should be "led as a lamb to the slaughter . . ."

Was the One of whom Isaiah spoke not walking the road to the cross when that prophetic word was uttered—and was rejected, as He would be when "He came unto His own, and His own received Him not"? *That* is the road to the cross.

3

From the Throne to the Manger

GOOD intentions are never a satisfactory substitute for the deeds they envisage. Indeed, it is often more bitter to know that promises were made and not kept, than it would have been if no anticipation had been aroused. The whole value of pledges of future action lies in their fulfilment. Therefore the promise of a Redeemer had to be followed by His accomplishing all that had been foretold. The Lamb slain from the foundation of the world had to become the Man of Calvary. The eternal purpose of redemption for mankind had to be wrought out in time. It was needful that Christ should be born of a virgin, in Bethlehem. The Son of God needs must be "made manifest in these last times" as our sin-bearer and Saviour.

Incidentally He exemplifies, in His humiliation, this great principle of Christian faith and experience, that profession without practice is vain. So many Christian people fail, in personal life and in witness for the Lord, at this point. They make the great mistake of assuming that a right attitude is all that is needful. Long ago, James declared bluntly that faith without works is dead; yet many still seem to regard correct doctrine, and mental assent to spiritual truth, as the essential reality of Christian faith. They need to learn anew the meaning of our Lord's words concerning His disciples, "By their fruits ye shall know them."

The identification of Christ with sinners and with their sin-offerings in the Old Testament dispensation, derived its value from the retrospective benefits of His Passion. He needs must fulfil in time the atoning purpose foreshadowed in every patriarchal and Levitical sacrifice. And so He came; and of necessity, He came to die. "Lo, I come (in the volume of the book it is written of me), to do Thy will, O God . . ." and that will found expression in the cross. He was walking that road ere ever His infant feet took their first faltering steps.

There is deep discernment expressed in the well-known picture of the boy Jesus, greeting the dawn in all the zest of early youth, with open arms; but the rising sun, in which He rejoices, throws a long shadow behind Him, like the shadow of a cross. The artist hints at the influence and foretaste of that coming event upon Him, even in childhood. But we can go farther back than that, and say that the shadow of the cross darkened the stable in which He was born, and fell across the manger in which the Babe was cradled.

He was born in Bethlehem because He was of David's royal line. That lineage was the proudest boast of both Joseph and Mary; and because of it—in accord with ancient promise—they were chosen by God for the highest privilege given to any human couple, of cherishing the Son of God incarnate. How eagerly they must have talked together about the angelic appearances and messages to them both, as they journeyed southward. The decree of Cæsar Augustus, which brought the young carpenter of Nazareth in Galilee, with his bride, to their ancestral home-town, accomplished the fulfilment of a higher decree, of a more lofty throne than that of the Emperor in Rome.

Yet in David's city, the heir of the House of David found no room, even in the inn: so the child was born in a place where cattle were kept, and their feeding-trough did duty as His cradle. Thus did Deity stoop, for the meeting of our human need.

How could heaven contain its adoring wonder at such surpassing love for fallen mankind! Angelic messengers proclaimed the good tidings of great joy, to shepherds who were watching their flocks by night on the foothills outside Bethlehem. And, guided by a star, wise men came from the east, bringing with them gifts of gold, and frankincense, and myrrh. Gold, yes; a most fitting gift for a new-born king. And frankincense, betokening that He was more than king of the Jews, but One to be worshipped: heaven's King, come, alas, to be despised and rejected of men. That surely is the significance of the myrrh—whatever might have been the thought of the giver in offering it. For myrrh is essentially associated with death; it was a chief spice used in embalming. Its solemn association with death invests it with symbolic significance as presented to the infant Christ: it re-emphasises that He was born in order to die. He came for this purpose: to give His life a ransom for many. The gift of myrrh indicated that His step from the throne to the manger was a step along the road to the cross.

Like every first-born son in Israel, Jesus was presented in the temple, by Joseph and Mary, when He was about six weeks old; and to the officiating priest, He was just another baby boy for whom the required offering was made, and the customary ceremony enacted. But there was in the House of God a Spirit-taught man who recognised in the Babe the long-promised Messiah—"Thy Salvation," he proclaimed Him, in thanksgiving to the Almighty. Then turning to the wondering mother, Simeon uttered strange and startling words: "Yea, a sword shall pierce through thy own soul also . . ."

That prophetic utterance forewarned Mary of an experience the full bitterness of which she could not possibly understand when it was spoken. It contains, however, profoundest implications for all who would be associated with the Lord as His disciples, as well as for the virgin mother. It intimated a suffering for and with the Lord, which all His followers share, in part. The "sword" which was to pierce Mary's bosom was largely the consequence of her own partial failure in faith; our "fellowship of His sufferings" will, conversely, be according to the measure of our faith. But the words of the aged seer in the temple declared from His earliest days an association with Him in suffering.

This leads us to the very heart of our theme: we seek, not merely to watch our Lord walk the road of the cross, that our emotions might be stirred and our devotion deepened; rather, we desire to *keep Him company* along that road. There is a sense in which He trod it alone: as our sin-bearer, our representative and substitute, He walked that way in absolute isolation. His was a solitary walk to the cross, as Redeemer of the race. In the paradox of faith, however, He invites us, as our Saviour and Lord, to walk that road with Him; to be identified with Him, as He identified Himself with us; to know the fellowship of His sufferings, being made comformable unto His death.

Let us then, not only during Lent and at Eastertide, but always, keep *Via Crucis* in view, not merely in remembrance of the road our Lord pursued and the redemption He accomplished, but as a present experience of fellowship with Him, accompanying Him in the way of the cross.

4

First Sight of the City

MODERN psychology has vastly increased our knowledge and understanding of human personality: but it cannot help in relation to the Person of our Lord. The Incarnation is a mystery apprehended by faith alone. How Jesus of Nazareth could be Very God and also truly Man, can never be explicitly defined. We can, of course, fully comprehend only what is within the range of our own experience: all beyond this must be accepted by faith or rejected in scepticism. This is true concerning the two natures united in the one Person of Jesus Christ. How could a helpless Babe be the almighty God? When did Jesus first realise that He was the Messiah? Where did His human limitations and His divine omnipotence meet? Such questions as these defy our best efforts to reduce this supreme manifestation and activity of Deity to the terms of our theological, philosophical or psychological systems of thought. Yet enough is revealed in the Word of God to inspire and nourish faith; enough to impart absolute assurance that Jesus was the Christ, the Son of the Blessed.

If we would keep Him company on the road to the cross, we must understand and enter into, as fully as possible, the period of preparation—the "silent years," as they are called—as well as the Messianic ministry of our Lord. There has been much speculation regarding His childhood, youth, and early manhood. Speculation it is, and must remain—except for the solitary incident recorded between His infancy and baptism by John in Jordan. That one incident, however, is remarkably illuminating, not only regarding Jesus Himself, but also concerning the manner of His upbringing in the home of Joseph and Mary in Nazareth.

Whether or not the mother ever spoke to her son about His wondrous birth, and the prophecies and strange events accompanying it, we are not told, and can never know. The impression given in the Gospel narratives, however, is that she preserved strict silence. She was adept at keeping her own counsel: more than once it is recorded that she "kept and pondered in her heart" matters evidently not discussed with anyone—not even with Joseph, who shared the experiences with her (e.g., Luke 2: 19, 51). Not a soul in Nazareth, save these two, apparently, knew anything about the incidents attendant upon Jesus' birth—or they would not have been so surprised and offended when He declared Himself to be the Messiah: their reaction was that of complete surprise that "one of themselves" should make such claims. "Is not this the carpenter's son?" they asked; "is not His mother called Mary? and His brethren, James, and Joses, and Simon, and Judas? and His sisters, are they not all with us? Whence then hath this man all these things?" (Matt. 13: 55, 56). Not a word was said about strange events accompanying His birth—and most certainly, any such stories would have been recalled instantly by someone, in a closely-knit community like Nazareth, if ever they had been current. The only explanation of the complete surprise, the total absence of any recollection of expectation and wondering concerning Him, is that Mary and Joseph had not revealed to a single person in the village the miracle of His birth and the prophecies made regarding Him.

Among the people whom He knew through childhood, therefore, right unto His full maturity, Jesus lived a normal and natural life. In the home, too, He was treated like any loved son of humble Israelites. It could not be otherwise. With the passing of the years, as He grew from infancy to boyhood, the thoughts and questionings and anticipations implanted in the minds of Joseph and Mary by the events of His birth, would gradually fade, and He would be regarded and treated just like the other children. For days, months—perhaps years— the fact that He was *not* just as the other members of the family might scarcely be remembered. He "increased in wisdom and stature" quite ordinarily; He went to the village synagogue-school, and learned to read and recite the Psalms and the Law. He helped in the house, and was taught to handle the tools in the carpenter's shop. Nothing was said, apparently, to the younger children of the family, about His distinction from them;

24

for, later, "neither did His brethren believe in Him"—they even went so far as to declare, "He is beside Himself" (Mark 3: 21); and Mary took sides with them against Him, so strongly had she suppressed her early "ponderings" and anticipations (Matt. 12: 46–50).

Thus He grew up, to outward seeming an ordinary village lad; and the time approached for His initiation into the responsibilities and privileges of an adult Israelite. At the age of 13 a Jewish boy became a "son of the law"—*Bar Mitzvar*—able to take part in the worship of temple and synagogue. Shortly before this, and as a preparation for it, Jesus was taken by Joseph and Mary to Jerusalem, presumably for the first time, on their annual visit for the Passover. What excitement, what eager enjoyment must have thrilled His whole being as He journeyed toward the Holy City! Every step of the way was redolent of sacred story; every hill and prospect had hallowed associations; every mile brought them nearer to Jerusalem itself, with its temple and stirring ceremonies!

All Jews, wherever they might be domiciled, were required by the Law to go up to Jerusalem thrice every year, for the three major feasts: in practice, however, this had proved impossible, and most of those living afar went only for the Passover. The journey from Galilee was more than a spiritual pilgrimage; it was also a great social event. Village folk would journey together; it would also be a time of reunion for families, scattered by marriage or for other reasons. In effect, this was to the people of Israel very largely what our summer holiday is to us: a time of change and refreshment, as well as of worship and spiritual exercise. The very journey itself was an adventure, with its "camping out" on the road: and to an imaginative youth, every moment had its thrills.

It is not difficult to enter into something of what this week in Jerusalem must have meant to the boy Jesus: His first sight of the splendours of the temple and its services; the elaborate ritual; the smoking sacrifice; the worshipping multitudes. The feast days sped by all too quickly; and then, amid orderly bustle the tents pitched just outside the city were struck, and the groups of laden pilgrims set off in differing directions on their homeward journeys. And among them, those of Nazareth in Galilee.

25

For a whole day they travelled, and only at nightfall did Joseph and Mary realise that Jesus was not in the party with which they were journeying. Their implicit trust in Him, that He would be in the place He ought to be, is deeply revealing: only on this occasion they had misunderstood where "the right place" for Him was. So, distressed concerning Him as they had never been since they had hastened from Bethlehem to Egypt at the command of an angel long years before, they retraced their weary steps to Jerusalem, and finally found Him on the third day—in the temple.

It was a most natural scene, most naturally told in Luke's Gospel: how the distraught couple saw the lad among the little crowd gathered round the rabbis who were giving public instruction, and their relief and weariness blended in Mary's eager words of remonstrance: "Son, why hast thou thus dealt with us? behold, thy father and I have sought thee sorrowing" (Luke 2: 48). Calmly, respectfully, lovingly, yet also with a deeper note, came the reply from the lips of the lad of twelve —"How is it that ye sought me? Wist ye not that I must be about my Father's business?"

Many questions are aroused by His action and this reply. Had He not known they were setting out on their journey home when they did? Had He deliberately given them this wearisome search and sustained anxiety? Was He, who after this incident returned home with them and was again "subject unto them" (v. 51), wilfully disobedient to their implicit, if not expressed, command, in order to effect some gracious purpose of His divine will? The Scriptures are silent on these deep issues; and speculation is vain. From His simple words, however, certain vastly important lessons may be learned; and the incident is recorded in order that we might do so.

First, the reply of Jesus is in the form of a question, "Wist ye not . . .?" This assumes that they should have known. There was something they had allowed to become obscure in their hearts and minds which should have been kept ever foremost; something had been practically forgotten which should have been cherished as a guiding principle of their thought and attitude concerning Him.

What was it, then, that they should have taken for granted, but which they had so neglected that it had virtually passed out of their reckoning? It was this . . . "that I must be about my Father's business." Now the literal translation of that phrase is, "in the things of my Father," or, in the colloquial language of today, "about my Father's affairs." Both the rendering of the A.V., and that of the R.V., "in my Father's House," paraphrase rather than translate the original Greek, as the I.V.F. *New Bible Commentary* points out. Jesus was surprised that Joseph and Mary did not understand that His Father's affairs should have first claim upon Him; should absorb and master Him. They had for so long regarded and treated Him just like an ordinary boy, and had so far forgotten that He was the Son of God, that even on this momentous first visit to the Holy City—except as a Babe in arms—affording Him His first contacts with the temple and its teachers, they took for granted that He would be just ordinarily interested, and be content to join the other village boys in the excitement of "packing up" and the fun of the homeward journey.

Whatever their attitude, the incident leaves us in no doubt that Jesus at the age of twelve had a full recognition of His divine Sonship. When and how this came to Him, is a much-debated point: personally, I believe it was a deep-seated realisation from His earliest infancy: part of the underlying consciousness of the realities of His existence, which deepened and strengthened as He "grew in wisdom and stature." It was of the very warp and woof of His Being; and the fact that Joseph and Mary did not *expect* Him to act accordingly, evoked His wondering questions, "How is it that ye sought me? Wist ye not that I must be about my Father's affairs?"

What, then, were His Father's affairs? In this instance, we are told: He had been engaged in the public discussions with the rabbinic teachers. It was the custom of the doctors of the law to hold disputations among themselves, for the public benefit, and also to impart instruction by means of question-and-answer methods, in the precincts of the temple, following the great religious festivals. There was nothing strange or unusual, then, in the fact of the lad asking and answering questions: the only occasion of surprise was the quality of "His understanding and His answers."

Now, while it is impossible to know for certain what subjects were discussed on this occasion—and there have been myriads of guesses—what would be more natural than that they should focus upon the ceremonies of the past few days; and that the boy Jesus should ask about the sacrifices He had seen offered for the first time in His life? Can we imagine Him discussing abstruse aspects of the Law—as some suggest—when His mind would naturally be teeming with thoughts about all that He had seen and heard in this past, most memorable week? He had witnessed, for the first time, the lamb slain and brought to the altar; the blood poured out; the offering burnt. Is it conceivable that He would not have countless questions to ask? Surely these were the "affairs of His Father" in which He would be absorbed.

They are, at least, the very heart of religion—of the Gospel, as well as of the old covenant: the meaning of the Passover; the significance of substitutionary sacrifice; the cleansing power of the shed blood; the atoning efficacy of the life presented on the altar; the consequent deliverance of the guilty Israelite from the penalty of his sin. For the boy in the temple, may we not be confident that these were the central concerns of His questions: and His "understanding" surely related to the fact that without the shedding of blood there is no remission.

How much more we should like to know about that discussion in the temple than we are told in Luke's restrained narrative; and whether or not the lad had any inkling that He was to offer in His own Person the one sacrifice for sins for ever—and thereby to impart to these animal sacrifices He had witnessed their true value? Certain it is that such understanding came to Him long before John the Baptist heralded Him as "the Lamb of God, which taketh away the sin of the world." Is it not reasonable to suggest, at least, that there was a shadow of the cross cast over that temple court more clearly defined than the shadow over the stable and the cradle of twelve years ago?

5

Numbered with the Transgressors

ALL Israel was on tiptoe of expectation. The herald of the Messiah had come, and was proclaiming that the Greater-than-he was at hand. No one doubted that John the Baptist was a prophet—the first for four hundred years. And an especial prophet: as he himself claimed, he was a voice inspired by God to call the nation to prepare a highway for His Anointed. In scorching words he summoned the people—from the highest in the land, and the very priests and rulers, to the rough soldiers and peasantry—unto repentance: to prepare themselves for the appearing of the Christ. He baptised the repentant in Jordan; but he told them plainly this was only a preparatory rite: One was coming who would baptise with the fire of the Holy Ghost.

John the Baptist perfectly fitted the Jewish conception of a prophet. Like Jeremiah and Ezekiel, he was a priest—at least, of priestly descent, though apparently not initiated into the priestly office, as he had gone instead into the wilderness, under the impulse of the Spirit, for the fulfilment of His prophetic ministry. He was dressed with dramatic simplicity, reminiscent of Elijah—indeed, in person and utterance he strongly resembled that great seer; and later, the One he heralded declared that John was in fact come in the spirit and power of Elijah, in fulfilment of ancient prophecy.

To a people agog with excitement and expectation, John declared that the coming of the Messiah was at hand. Not that they expected, for a moment, one such as Jesus of Nazareth: on the contrary, they dreamed of another Judas Maccabæus, a military leader and national hero, who would lead a successful uprising against the Romans, and throw off once for all the hated foreign yoke. Besotted with arrogant conceptions of their destiny as the chosen nation, they indulged in fantastic day-dreams of humbling the proud legions of Rome, and themselves exalted over all the peoples of the earth. It was with fervid eagerness, therefore, that they awaited the indication of the Lord's Anointed—a Saul in stature and prowess, and a David in kingly qualities. And so they gathered daily in great numbers, of all ranks of society, around the austere preacher on Jordan's banks.

At last, one day the tense vigil was ended; the finger of the prophet was pointed, and he uttered the thrilling words, "This is He of whom I spake!" But as the crowds turned jubilantly to gaze at the young man to whom John pointed, they instantly were filled with consternation: they saw at a glance that He was no Maccabæus. And John's exclamation, "Behold the Lamb of God, which taketh away the sin of the world," made them look at one another dumbfounded. What language was this, concerning a Messiah and Deliverer! They wanted a King, not a Lamb! In that moment they took *their* first step on the road that led to the cross—that cross to which they would relentlessly harry and hound Him and on which they would taunt Him.

A strange incident had occurred shortly before this event— just how long before we are not quite sure, but while John was baptising, this same young man had come quietly forward among those desiring to submit themselves to the rite. Whether or not the Baptist knew his cousin we cannot say; nor are we told whether or not he knew of the miraculous events and inspired words concerning his own birth and that of his cousin. But this we know: that as the two now came face to face, John recognised that here was One quite different from every other applicant for baptism; and he impulsively exclaimed, "I have need to be baptised of Thee, and comest Thou to me?" To which Jesus made the seemingly strange reply, "Suffer it to be so now: for thus it becometh us to fulfil all righteousness."

Alone of all who had stepped into the waters of Jordan, Jesus made no confession of sin, and gave no indication of repentance. John saw in Him an unsullied righteousness; a loftier dedication than his own. He who had rebuked a nation now bowed his head in submission; he who had baptised would fain be baptised. The greatest of all the prophets recognised One who was greater still; the herald beheld his Lord.

Impelled by this Spirit-taught consciousness, John wished to change places with the newcomer; but with quiet authority He exclaimed, "Suffer it to be so now . . ." Thus John, obedient to His command, baptised his Lord; and thus the sinless Son of God incarnate was numbered with the transgressors. For John's baptism was essentially "unto repentance"; it was an enacted confession of sin, and of desire for cleansing and pardon.

But why should the spotless One present Himself among the sullied and the guilty? Because He had "left His throne and kingly crown" for this very purpose; and, moreover, not merely to take His place *among* them, but to *take their place*, substitutionally; to bear their guilt and to pay their penalty, as the representative of a sinful race. In the very act which initiated His public ministry as Messiah He embraced and foreshadowed the death He would suffer on the cross, that repentant sinners might indeed be pardoned and cleansed.

Jesus "fulfilled all righteousness" in committing Himself to the accomplishing of the redeeming purpose of God, whereby a "gift of righteousness" could be bestowed on sinful men. But first, He must take His place as the representative guilty One; and so, He identified Himself with sinners in the waters of baptism. It was an essential first step in that stretch of the road to the cross which He must tread in the full public gaze, during His Messianic ministry. And the seal of God the Father upon it came in the voice from heaven: "Thou art my beloved Son; in Thee I am well pleased"—a remarkable linking of phrases from Psalm 2: 7 and Isaiah 42: 1 which portray Jesus as the Messianic Son and the Suffering Servant. "The path to Calvary," observes Dr. Ralph P. Martin, "runs from Jordan's river."

How strange and tragic it is that controversy should have rent the Church and divided asunder devout followers of the Lord, concerning the very aspects of our faith which should most unite and bind us together—the sacrament He instituted to mark initiation into His Kingdom, and that to be observed in remembrance of His death. It is far from our present purpose to become involved in such controversy, but we would observe the deep significance of baptism by immersion—as, by almost universal agreement, John practised and Jesus experienced it in Jordan.

There could be no symbolic act more expressive of death and burial and resurrection, than baptism by immersion. Its implications can be clearly discerned by the simplest observer. The consequence of sin is defilement, and the penalty of sin is death. The repentant sinner acknowledges his guilt and is aware of his doom; and in distress of heart and mind he seeks a place of repentance, of pardon and of cleansing. But in the divine economy, pardon can be found only as the penalty is borne: death alone can deal with sin.

That is why Christ came, and died for us: taking our guilt, He paid our penalty and died our death. He identified Himself with us in order that we might become identified with Him in His resurrection-triumph. He took our place in Jordan, that we might find forgiveness and receive eternal life.

But we too must walk the road to the cross: we must reckon ourselves to be dead indeed unto sin, and alive unto God through Jesus Christ our Lord. For we are buried with Him by baptism into death, that like as Christ was raised up from the dead by the glory of the Father, even so we also should walk in newness of life. Said the apostle Paul, "I am crucified with Christ: nevertheless I live; yet no longer I, but Christ liveth in me . . ."

He walked the road to the cross for us, deliberately, firmly, without stumbling or halting. And now, from the throne where, as glorified and exalted Man, He is our representative and great High Priest, He invites us, in a fellowship of love and devotion, to walk with Him along the way of self-renouncing and of life through death. For be assured of this: walk the road to the cross we must, either as His companions or as His enemies; either in the fellowship of His sufferings, being made conformable unto His death, or else crying, "Crucify Him! Away with Him! We will not have this Man to reign over us!" This is an inescapable "either—or."

6

Face to Face with the Devil

TEMPTATION is something that we all know so much about, that it is not surprising the story of our Lord's temptation in the wilderness holds such a fascination for us. That encounter with the devil stirs our imagination, and we wonder how we should fare had we to meet him in single combat under such stark conditions. It is profoundly strengthening to us, in all our lesser temptations, to know that He who was, in His incarnation, tempted in all points like as we are, triumphed gloriously. His victory was achieved through steadfast faith, and the wielding of the sword of the Spirit, which is the Word of God. These are the means of victory for us, also.

Jesus was tempted in a twofold capacity: as Man, and as Messiah. The temptations were real and fierce, to Him personally. He was ravenously hungry; He was burning with intense desire that the people should believe on Him and heed His word; His yearning for mankind reached out unto all the kingdoms of the world. Satan offered Him the satisfaction of these strong desires: and to His true human nature the temptation was insidious. Vastly more was dependent upon His resisting the tempter, however, than His personal experience as man: the ministry He was about to begin as Messiah was also dependent upon it. Of course, His personal experience and Messianic office were inextricably bound up, and we cannot separate them, even in thought: the entire redeeming purpose of God in sending His Son to be the Saviour of men was involved in His response to the tempter. He was there as representative man: the second Adam. As Adam fell, and in falling brought upon the race the entail of sin and death, so Christ in His victory provides a way of deliverance for all who trust in Him.

Part of the severity of the testing lay in the fact that Jesus was *alone* with the devil in the wilderness. Perils are accentuated when we confront them alone. We are foolish to give the devil this advantage over us, if we can avoid it. The "fellowship of kindred minds" can banish many a temptation! There are times, however, when we cannot escape single combat with the enemy. Therefore our Lord—the Captain of our salvation—also faced him alone. And since no one else was there, it is clear that Jesus Himself must afterwards have told His disciples the details of this ordeal. He wished them, and us, to know that He was tempted—and therefore not only understands the ferocity of the devil's onslaughts, but also is able to succour them that are tempted. Moreover, through this record of His experience He wished to teach us vital lessons concerning the wiles of the devil, and how to combat them. Our Lord's temptations, fierce as they were to Him individually, were yet "patterns" of the various types of temptations we meet: and in resisting them He not only triumphed over the adversary, but indicated for all time the way of escape. For, like Him, we are tempted both in our personal life and in relation to the purpose and service of God. There are temptations which we share with all mankind, and others which come to us specifically as Christians. In all these, we can "find grace to help" from the Man who is our Mediator on high.

The *timing* of the temptation is significant: it immediately followed His baptism. The long years of quiet preparation were ended: the herald had proclaimed to the nation that its Messiah had come. His self-dedication in Jordan had been sealed by the voice from heaven expressing the Father's good pleasure. And straightway—to use the word beloved by Mark —He was led (or *driven* is Mark's strong word) by the Spirit into the wilderness. . . . So often we, too, experience an onslaught of the devil following an act of dedication or a season of especial spiritual blessing. We may be assured that *we* are never driven by the Spirit into temptation, for our Lord Himself taught us to pray, "Lead us not into temptation"; but this story gives us the reassurance that when we meet the tempter, even his fiercest testing is under the governance of the Spirit of God; for all that happens to the child of God is within the compass of His over-ruling will. Our Lord's temptation, however, was not only allowed but precipitated by the Spirit, before He began His public ministry: it was One empowered through resistance and conquest over the tempter, who went forth to preach and to teach. How wise the Church would be if it followed more closely the example of the Lord in this respect!

The three temptations were directed through three avenues of approach—the physical, religious, and spiritual. They exemplify the whole range of temptation, experienced by all mankind. They make their appeal to body, soul, and spirit.

Hunger is expressive of our physical, material and temporal needs and desires: and these include all that today we sum up in the term, our *standard of living*—or, colloquially, "keeping up with the Joneses." What temptations come to us along these lines: the satisfaction of our wants, and of our craving for possessions. Within this category most of the temptations of the majority of mankind are embraced. Over against this insatiable demand of our appetites and desires, the Lord sets forth the standard of divine requirement, and also the way of deliverance: man does not live by bread—the satisfaction of human cravings—alone; he is spirit as well as body, and vastly more vital and satisfying is to know and obey the Word of God. But, in "temptation's evil hour," when the desires of the flesh are so impelling, how can we find the strength to turn from them and to heed the Word of the Lord? Frankly, we cannot hope to prevail through obedience to that Word *as law*, any more than Adam did: but since the Word became incarnate, and overcame the tempter in our likeness and on our behalf, and is with us and in us, to strengthen and inspire heart and mind and will, what would be impossible to us "in Adam" becomes possible—and wondrously our own true experience—"in Christ." Identified with Him, through faith, we prove the reality of His identification with us in every time of testing and of need. He makes His triumph ours, and gives us the victory through His strengthening grace.

To the temptations which come to us as sons of Adam, however, are added those which we meet as Christians. In matters of religion, we delight in something so dramatic as casting ourselves from a pinnacle of the temple, that the Lord might bear us up. . . . We crave supernatural confirmation of our faith;

and we delight in sensuous, exultant experiences, instead of the exercise of simple trust. How much of deviation from the simplicity of the Scriptures and of New Testament practice is comprehended within this temptation. It accounts for all the extremes of sensationalism and ritualism found in the various groupings of the professing Church. The stern word of Jesus concerning all that presumes upon His grace, and perverts the meaning of His revealed will, is—"Thou shalt not tempt the Lord thy God." Trust is the key-word concerning discipleship; single-minded faith is the answer to this deceit of the devil.

Finally—and we are following the order given by Matthew, though Luke reverses the last two—the devil endeavoured to enthral our Lord with a panoramic view of the kingdoms of the world and the glory of them. Few people have not at some time or other felt the attraction and lure of the world. All too often, it is to our baser natures that its appeal is strongest: in our Lord's case, of course, "the world," as we use the term, would have no attraction at all. But He had come to this earth in fulfilment of the compassionate grace of the Father, who "so loved the world that He gave His only-begotten Son . . ." and the subtle suggestion of the tempter was that He could achieve His purpose for the world in a moment, by one act of homage to the tempter—and thus He would avoid the cross, which would be rendered unnecessary. How great a goal to attain at so small a cost! What folly it would be not to seize upon it: to set the world free from the entail of sin, at the cost of one mere act of homage! But therein lay the demonic character of the temptation: there could be no such thing as a "mere act of homage," for the very fact of falling down and worshipping the devil would bring the worshipper under his dominion. It is impossible to accept what the devil offers of the kingdoms of the world and the glory of them, without coming under his authority and control. We may think we are receiving benefit at his hands, only to find we have surrendered ourselves into his satanic grasp. He offers to give, in order to gain; he promises the world and its glamour, but we find ourselves instead in his chains.

There is one way of escape, and it is indicated in the un-equivocal response of Jesus—"Get thee hence, Satan: for it is written, Thou shalt worship the Lord thy God, and Him only shalt thou serve."

Thus the temptations of the wilderness, besides the vindication they afford of the unsullied sinlessness of Jesus, and His qualification to become our great High Priest, represent all the devious devices with which the adversary of our souls would entrap us, at every stage of life and in every aspect of our experience. A dominant note in them all is the casting of doubt upon our Father's grace and power: "If God is Almighty and you are His child, then why . . . ?" Nothing can more speedily and effectually mar our fellowship with God, and shatter our peace, than to harbour such thoughts. The very quintessence of faith, on the other hand, is to "trust where it cannot see." Equally insidious is the inducement to presume upon our relationship to Him as sons of God, and upon His bounty as our heavenly Father. "If we are His sons, then why shouldn't we act daringly . . ." but that can lead us into every imaginable extravagance and presumption. And the third strand in the "threefold cord" of temptation is the misquotation of Scripture, to make our yielding to temptation seem reasonable and right, instead of downright sinning!

Our one means of safety is revealed in the manner of our Lord's dealing with all three temptations: a comprehensive and sound and Spirit-taught knowledge and understanding of the Word of God; a discernment between faith and presumption; an unhesitating rejection of wrong, however attractive it might appear to be. But who of us could so act, in every time of testing? It is because of our inability and insufficiency that Jesus submitted to temptation: that, perfected as our Saviour through such experience, He might be in us, our sufficiency and our strength in all our "wilderness" days and hours.

Jane Austen, that shrewd delineator of human character, in her greatest novel, *Pride and Prejudice*, unfolds the story of the love of the patrician Fitzwilliam Darcy for Elizabeth Bennet, despite the social inferiority of her family. The climax which revealed the true depth and lofty steadfastness of his love, was his condescending to meet and make terms with the profligate Wickham, who had deceived and maligned him and seduced Elizabeth's frivolous sister Lydia. Darcy brought himself to endure and effect what was most distasteful to him, in order to rescue Elizabeth from ignominy. But divine truth is even stranger than fiction's most astounding flights of fancy; for the only-begotten Son of God, the Effulgence of His glory and the express Image of His Person, stooped, out of love for fallen man, the creature of dust, to meet the adversary who had rebelled and maligned Him—not, indeed, to come to terms with him, but to submit to his most subtle and strong temptations. This He did for love of us, to rescue us from ignominy and doom, and to deliver us in the hour of peril.

There is, however, a yet deeper bond of fellowship between the Lord and His people, in the time of temptation, exemplified in the relationship between Jesus and the Twelve. While the wilderness ordeal was endured in loneliness, it was not the sum-total of temptation that He experienced: the devil attacked Him—as he does us—constantly, in manifold ways and guises. And in many of these the apostles participated, so that He could say to them, in the Upper Room, "ye are they which have continued with me in my temptations"—and manifestly He said this with gratitude, and in acknowledgement of the fact that their fellowship had been a comfort to Him. How inspiring it is to know that, frail and faulty men as they were, nevertheless they were companions of Christ in His temptations. He had met the devil *alone*, and overcome him; but He valued their companionship when they could give it—and in that, as in other aspects of relationship to the Lord, they were representative of all His disciples. It is a Christ who knows the comfort of companionship in testing, who pledges never to leave us alone in any time of temptation.

It was through yielding to temptation that Adam fell, and brought upon all mankind the reign of sin and death. That transgression in Eden involved the race, and necessitated that the Redeemer should suffer the sorrows of the road to the cross. Henceforth every son of Adam would experience the discomfiture of defeat and the penalty of guilt. The Son of Man was the one exception to the long, sad story of succumbing to sin: in the weakness of His true humanity He met the tempter in all the subtlety and ferocity of his assault—and He triumphed gloriously. It behoved Him, in accomplishing our salvation, in all things to be made like unto His brethren, that He might be a merciful and faithful High Priest. . . . For in that He

Himself hath suffered being tempted, He is able to succour them that are tempted. . . . For we have not an high priest which cannot be touched with the feeling of our infirmities; but was in all points tempted like as we are, yet without sin. Let us therefore come boldly unto the throne of grace . . . (Heb. 2: 17, 18; 4: 15, 16).

Temptation therefore, the occasion of so much sin and shame and sorrow, is over-ruled for the Christian by the Holy Spirit, impelling him into closer communion with the Lord; into a deeper consciousness of dependence and greater constancy of trust. He knows that the cross is the one means of deliverance and victory; that walking with the Lord in the way of the cross is the one secret of triumph over temptation. That which the enemy designs for our downfall becomes instead the means of his own; it is transmuted into the very instrument for the perfecting of the purposes of God in us, in dependence upon the One who suffered being tempted, that He might succour His people in every temptation within the range of human experience.

7

Companions for the Way

JESUS set great store by the men He chose to keep Him company in the way—along that road which led, although they so little realised it until near the end, to the cross. Companionship is one of the fundamental needs of human nature. There are, of course, misanthropes who prefer seclusion to fellowship with other people: but these are either abnormal, or have chosen the life of a recluse for religious or other purposes. There was in Jesus of Nazareth no trait or tendency that would alienate Him from His fellows—except His single-minded devotion to the will of God, which angered the ungodly and the hypocritical. One of His first activities as the Messiah was to invite to follow Him—to keep Him company in the way, as Dr. Campbell Morgan liked to render the command, *akolouthei moi*—that motley band of men who became the apostles. In choosing them, He not only desired to train them for the great tasks ahead, but also He wanted their friendship.

Too often, perhaps, we under-estimate the value which God places upon the love and devotion of His people. It is true that we owe all we have and are to Him: we cannot too strongly stress the wonder of His grace toward us, and our condition of utter dependence upon Him. But having loved and redeemed us, and shed abroad His love in our hearts, He looks for responding love and ever-deepening devotion on our part. There is something which His people can render to God Most High, which He values far above the flawless worship of the angelic host. And in His humiliation, Jesus our Lord longed for the loyal allegiance and human affection of Peter and James and John, and other quite ordinary folk. He was their Lord and Leader; they came in time to realise that He was their Saviour and God: but in the fleeting months of His public ministry they were His associates and helpers, and—with all their imperfections and slowness of spiritual apprehension—Jesus found in their companionship and devotion an inexpressible comfort and strength. They, privileged above all men in being His companions as He walked the roads and field-paths of Palestine, were also file-leaders of the great army of disciples who, through faith, in all the succeeding centuries have sought to walk with Him on the road to the cross.

Who and what, then, were these friends of the Christ? We know practically nothing about some of them, except their names. What is evident is that they comprised a cross-section of the people of their day, and were truly representative of all men of faith, of every age and of every clime. If *they* could walk with Jesus, so can we. They varied in age, in temperament, in capacities and qualities. Some were summoned to follow by the Lord Himself; others were invited by kinsfolk or friends, to come to Him. Most emphatically they were not religious fanatics, or even surpassingly devout. They were sincere, godly folk, of quite ordinary character and abilities. Some were forthright, blusterous extroverts, like Peter; others, contemplative like John and Nathanael; one at least, Simon the Zealot, had been involved in political agitation against the Romans, while another had been prepared to serve the conquerors as a tax-gatherer; some were moody and inclined to be pessimistic, like Thomas; others were kindly and reticent, like Philip. All were aspiring for places of privilege in Messiah's kingdom, and became disciples of Jesus with their own ambitions in view, as well as thoughts of service they could render Him. The Master chose no starry-eyed band, thirsting to spend and be spent in the cause to which they had dedicated themselves: just average, self-seeking, yet sincere and God-fearing men, of differing qualities, but united by this great bond of companionship with the Christ on the road to the cross.

He led them along with gentle authority and kingly grace, which bound their hearts to Him with ever-strengthening cords of love and esteem—that is, in the case of all save one, who grew increasingly bitter and antagonistic as it became clearer that his worldly ambitions would not be realised, and who accordingly sought the recompense of the reward of treachery, in the thirty pieces of silver.

At first all had seemed to them to go so well. Great crowds thronged round Jesus as He wrought miracles and spoke so enthrallingly that "all bare Him witness, and wondered at the gracious words which proceeded out of His mouth." The Twelve felt themselves to be important people indeed, as His intimate acquaintances. But there were puzzling incidents: He seemed to miss opportunities of becoming the national hero-deliverer; and there were conflicts with the priests and other authorities which were disturbing to their aspirations. Then came a day when He spoke so strangely—of His flesh as bread and His blood as drink; and that, apart from eating and drinking these, no one could have true life—that many of His followers declared they couldn't understand, and couldn't associate themselves with Him any longer. In consternation the Twelve saw the great majority of the crowd which had been following as His avowed disciples, depart. And when Jesus turned to them and asked, bluntly, "Will you also go away?" they looked at one another embarrassed, scarcely knowing what to think or how to reply; and they were relieved when Peter, impetuous as usual, spoke up and said, "Lord, to whom shall we go? Thou hast the words of eternal life." They *had* been perplexed; they *had* wondered what to do: but in their inmost hearts they knew that, even when they couldn't understand, His words were true, and struck the deepest chords within them. He had won their love and loyalty so completely that they could not seriously consider, even for a moment, forsaking Him: they would keep Him company on this road, lead where it might.

That was, perhaps, their first act of true self-dedication in discipleship: the deliberate pledging of themselves to His cause, without primary consideration of their own ambition and advantage. This new devotion was soon put to the test: for it became increasingly manifest that the established leaders of Israel were—far from acclaiming Him, and rallying to His cause—hostile, seeking to confound and defame Him, and bring Him into disfavour with the people. On the one hand, they saw the miracles and heard the words of grace and truth which left them in no doubt that He was the Messiah; on the other, it was now quite apparent that the chief priests and rulers would not acknowledge Him as such. The situation had become ominous and full of peril: dreams of His being acclaimed the greater king than David began to fade, and their own prospects of place and prosperity to diminish.

Together with these disturbing developments, were strange remarks which Jesus was making. "If any man will come after me, let him deny himself, and take up his cross daily, and follow me . . ." His *cross?* The very word made one shudder! What could the Lord mean by such language as this? It evoked thoughts of disgrace and intolerable anguish. In plain terms, it could mean only one thing: death. Yet Jesus had spoken of taking up a cross *daily:* of living death, of daily dying. Dimly they apprehended that He who so frequently spoke in parables was doing so now: that He meant a life of self-denial; indeed, a veritable dying to self. But they could not quite make it out, and preferred not to think too much about it.

Then came a decisive day, at Cæsarea Philippi, when Jesus confronted them plainly with a question they had long puzzled over and often debated among themselves: "Whom say ye that I am?" Once again Peter spoke for them all: "Thou art the Christ, the Son of the living God." Having been with Him so intimately, having seen and heard all He did and said, in public and in private, through these past eventful months, they could come to no other conclusion. And the glowing face of the Lord, as He replied, "Blessed art thou, Simon Bar-jona: for flesh and blood hath not revealed it unto thee, but my Father which is in heaven," brought a responding glow in their hearts; and, somewhat awed by the very confession they had made, and its implications, they nevertheless knew in their hearts that it was true. And from that time on, Jesus spoke clearly of what lay ahead—not public recognition and acclaim, but rejection and crucifixion. The road they were treading, they now began to realise more starkly, would lead to the cross. And it was Thomas who this time spoke for them all, when he said, "Let us also go, that we may die with Him."

In spite of all this, they were unprepared for what was entailed in accompanying the Lord to the very end. Who can blame them? They had to meet, on that road, not only the basest passions and depravities of men, but also the fiercest onslaught of hell. We can only marvel at and admire their

43

steadfast purpose of loyalty and devotion. The Lord did not under-estimate their self-denying love to Him, nor their true comradeship—despite all their very human frailties—in the way He was called to tread. He knew that, in its most bitter aspect, He must walk it alone: but He fain would have their company insofar as they could give it. This yearning for their companionship was supremely manifest in the Garden, when He urged them to ". . . watch with me"; and later, finding them sleeping, He said, in tones of sad rebuke, "Could ye not watch with me one hour?"—but hastened to add, lest His words should wound them too grievously, "the spirit indeed is willing, but the flesh is weak." Even amid the agony which caused Him to sweat as it were great drops of blood, He indicated His understanding of their human weakness and limitations, and spoke words of compassionate grace. Yet He had longed for their fellowship in watching and in prayer in that hour of His ultimate travail as man, in submitting to the will of the Father and the death of the cross.

The story of our Lord's relationship with His disciples comes to all who would follow in their train, with inspiration and challenge. Much as we need the Lord, in His redeeming ministry and High Priestly office, this also is true, that He has need of us. He who keeps us company in all the changing scenes of life, invites us to keep Him company in the way of the cross. As to the Twelve of old, He calls us to be His friends; to love and serve and obey Him, in all that true fellowship involves. Only so can we be His witnesses unto the end of the earth, in the power of His resurrection.

8

Decisive Cross-roads

IN THE experience of every one of us there are critical decisions we have to make which determine the whole course and
character of life. These are the factors which shape our
destiny: they govern the whole pattern of life, and their effects
find expression in practically every event of every day. Some
such decisions may be effected once for all: the critical choice
being made, the matter is settled for ever. In other cases,
decisions firmly taken have to be adhered to, by a process of
constant reaffirmation. That is true of all decisions relating to
the spiritual life of the Christian believer: certain issues have
to be determined by a deliberate choice, yet that choice must
be ratified by faith repeatedly. Faith is the life-breath of
Christianity; it is the steady persistence of trust in God, and
continual receiving of His grace in Jesus Christ our Lord. The
act of faith by which we first received Him as Saviour and
Lord, initiates a life of relationship with Him, obedience to
Him, and dependence upon Him.

> High heaven that heard that solemn vow,
> That vow renewed shall daily hear. . . .

In His humiliation, our Lord submitted Himself to the conditions of our human life; as Son of man He lived and walked by
faith. He is the example, as well as the source, of faith, for all
His people. For Him, as for all mankind, there were great decisions which, once taken, fixed His future course: nevertheless
each step in the chosen way had to be taken by faith and in
obedience to the will of His Father.

Now, there were some such vital issues in the life of our Lord
of which we have no information: and speculation concerning
them is worse than vain. We have hints in Scripture of His

embracing the will of the Father before time began; the initial setting of His feet on the road to the cross, in submission to the eternal decrees. Then, in the fulness of time, He entered our earthly scene, by means of the Incarnation. "Lo, I come," He declared, in accordance with the prophetic word, "in the volume of the book it is written of me, to do Thy will, O God." We have a glimpse of Him as a lad of twelve, absorbed in the affairs of His Father; and we see Him at the age of thirty going into the waters of Jordan to identify Himself with the sinners He had come to redeem—His deliberate acceptance and foreshadowing of the death He was to endure. Somewhere between these two events there had come to Him as man the full realisation of the character of the ministry He was to fulfil: and as man, He made His own that revealed will of God, albeit the end was the cruel cross.

For Jesus of Nazareth, as for us all, the full implications of obedience to the will of God were set forth in the Scriptures. The cross He was to endure had been described in graphic terms by psalmists and prophets, and symbolised in the sacrifices of the old covenant. He knew the road He was treading. So should every disciple who would walk in His steps. No one is ever lured by God into Christian profession and discipleship, through the imparting of false impressions and the raising of false hopes: the true character and costliness of the Christian life are plainly declared in the Word of God. If anyone fails to understand these, it is through limited understanding of the Scriptures, or through hearing a faulty presentation of the Gospel message—as, we must acknowledge, often occurs in evangelistic services and meetings. We do despite to the Gospel, however, and render grave disservice to the hearers, when only the wooing note of the Evangel is sounded forth, and its admonitions to count the cost are neglected. We share with all mankind, of course, the vicissitudes and vagaries of life; though for the Christian these become subject to the divine over-ruling, so that we can rest in the assurance that all things work together for good to them that love God. Concerning our discipleship, specifically, the Lord Jesus said that if we would follow Him we must be ready to walk in the way of the cross. And we may be quite sure that what is so plainly set before us, was no less clearly set before Him, when as man He made that irrevocable inward self-dedication to the will of His Father. From that time onward, Jesus of Nazareth was consciously walking the road to the cross. There followed other critical decisions: but these were all in the nature of reaffirmations of the great choice which had been made once for all, rather than complementary decisions. Yet each one was a sharp testing, an occasion for the devil to use all his blandishments and his devices; each called for faith and fortitude and highest courage —that courage which, while it is the expression of trust in God on the part of the one who displays it, is nevertheless inspired by the Spirit of God.

We have already witnessed two of these critical occasions, in which our Lord ratified His dedication to the will of the Father, and committed Himself by deliberate act to the fulfilling of that will—first, in Jordan; and second, in His rejection of every subtle suggestion of the devil, in the wilderness, that He should side-step the cross. These were swiftly followed by another, when He "returned in the power of the Spirit to Galilee." He taught in the synagogues, and "a fame of Him went throughout all the region," Luke records; adding that He was "glorified of all." This was a propitious beginning: the scene was set, surely, for a glorious triumph for His message and ministry. But Luke proceeds to tell how, in His first recorded sermon—in the synagogue of His own village of Nazareth—Jesus read from Isaiah 61 : 1, 2, and affirmed that this passage from the prophecy was that very day fulfilled in their ears. "And all bare Him witness, and wondered at the gracious words which proceeded out of His mouth." Here was a response to warm His heart! But He had more to say—and as He spoke, their gratified and gracious looks gave place to astonishment, which in turn changed to consternation, and quickly passed into anger. At last they could listen no longer, and rising up they thrust Him out of the synagogue and out of the city, and led Him to the brow of the hill on which the city was built, that they might cast Him down headlong. Only by a seeming miracle was He able, by passing through the midst of them, to escape their murderous intentions.

What caused this startling change of attitude, from patronising complacency to raging fury? Simply a few home truths! Jesus had told them that it was not enough to murmur pleasing compliments upon His address: they needed to attend, to take His words to heart, and to obey. It was not enough to be gratified that a "local boy" could preach well: they should heed the word which God had spoken through His lips. He reminded them how their forefathers had, through an attitude of familiarity toward the prophets, neglected to obey their word—and missed the blessing God was seeking to bestow, but which strangers had experienced, in their stead. It was this hint that God might pass them by, and grant His grace to the Gentiles instead, which evoked their indignation and rage.

It is easy to find excuses for these people of Nazareth. They had been well disposed to the young preacher, and quite complimentary in their commendation of His discourse. Surely it would have been wiser to let them disperse in that spirit of complacency, and to seek gradually to build upon that initial goodwill, leading them gently from one truth to another as they were able to receive it? That at least, would be the counsel of worldly-wisdom—alas, all too familiar among Christian people and Christian communities today. The Lord would have none of it. He had not come to tickle man's ears, and to woo by guile their good opinion and condescending approval of His teaching. He had come to declare the whole counsel of God. He had come to show men their own hearts and minds and lives as God regards them. He had come to reveal the true need of every heart and life, and the heavenly Father's provision to meet it. If they had no sense of need, however; if they were so pleased with themselves as to be impervious to the word of divine warning or admonition; if they sat in judgment upon His word rather than recognising its judgment of them, then bludgeoning bluntness of speech was necessary, in order to bring home to them their blind folly. As the messenger of God, our Lord Jesus could not allow them to continue in self-deception, smug and serene, while their condition in the sight of God was perilous. He must stab them awake to spiritual realities, cost what it might. The responsibility for acceptance or rejection of the shattering truth, would then firmly rest on their own shoulders.

Men and women do not like to be jostled out of their self-complacency: they react violently today, as they did then. Alas, they are not often thus disturbed, in their sleep of spiritual death. There are few disciples of the Lord who follow in the steps of the Master in this respect; few who proclaim to men in burning words the truth concerning themselves, concerning sin and judgment, concerning heaven and hell, concerning the issues involved in reaction to the Word of God. Preachers prefer honeyed words today, to the forthright speech of Jesus of Nazareth; to lead people gently on, rather than to startle them into stark awareness of spiritual realities. Tragically, leading them gently on seldom brings them into the Kingdom of God; it is all too often a synonym for complacent stagnation. The last thing we must do, however, is to offend a hearer! Have we not heard re-echoed, when a faithful preacher speaks as did his Lord in Nazareth, some such exclamations as were probably uttered in the synagogue that day—"We were all quite happy in our synagogue until He came, with His disturbing talk and accusing manner, almost as if we were *heathen*! Why, the very fact that we attend the synagogue regularly shows that we are God-fearing people. How He dared to say such things about *us*, we cannot imagine. . . ." But despite it all, they were deaf to the voice of God, and neglectful of His Word—and violently angry when the Son of God told them the truth about their lifeless and barren religiosity. At their hands He suffered His first experience of physical violence. It was the first manifestation of the spirit which would pursue Him henceforward, until its final achievement in bringing Him to the cross.

What happened in Nazareth was repeated on a larger scale in relation to the nation as a whole, and especially the chief priests and rulers. The people gladly listened to the Lord while He told enthralling parables, and were agog while He wrought miracles: but when He spoke of sin and righteousness and judgment; of repentance and faith and obedience, they were resentful. We read repeatedly of their taking up stones to stone Him (John 8: 59; 10: 31, 39). As for the rulers, they were incensed at His scornful exposure of the hypocrisy of their manifold observances which were a mere façade behind which they hid their exploitation of religion for selfish ends. Again, would it not have been politic to win the good opinion of these influential men, and educate them into nobler thoughts and better ways, rather than antagonising them, and provoking them to an opposition which found its ultimate expression in the cross? But never in a thousand years would even the Christ have succeeded in reforming these hardened and guileful sinners, and transforming them gradually into true men of God. They were blind leaders of the blind; arrogant in their hypocritical guise of godliness; accomplishing evil by their influence and example, as well as by calculated misdeed; defaming and disgracing the Name of God, which they so readily and so sacrilegiously took upon their lips. There was only one thing to be done: to expose their falsehood, and to present, in contrast to their travesty of true religion, the verity of vital faith in the holy and living God. But by stripping off their mask, Jesus earned their implacable hatred; by exposing their evil, He evoked their enmity toward Himself—and set them planning to send Him to the cross.

More than once it seemed that antagonism against Him had reached a murderous pitch, and must result in a fatal assault; and on several such occasions Jesus withdrew to the wilderness, to allow passions to cool: for He knew that His time had not yet come. He was proceeding steadfastly on the road to the cross, according to His Father's will: yet nothing must be allowed to precipitate the appointed hour. The Pascal Lamb must be offered at Jerusalem, at the feast of the Passover. But as the hour drew near, He went up to that feast. A message came from Bethany, concerning a friend who was sick. "Surely You are not going to Judæa again?" the disciples exclaimed: "don't You remember how the Jews tried to stone You when You were last there?" But it was not merely the need of the family at Bethany which drew Him thither—though the raising of Lazarus had its place in the developing drama of events. It was, supremely, to give Himself unto the death of the cross— to which the calling of the brother of Martha and Mary from the tomb was incidental—that our Lord journeyed from the safety of the desert to the perils of the city: that city which was so far to depart from the divine intention expressed in its name, the Holy City, as to perpetrate the most dreadful deed of all history.

In Jerusalem, during that final week of conflict with the rulers, Jesus passed the last of these "decisive cross-roads," when He pronounced against the religious hierarchy the most devastating denunciation of men ever uttered. "Woe unto you,

50

scribes and pharisees, hypocrites . . ." The stinging, searing words were repeated again and again, as He brought against them a series of indictments which stripped them of all their sham and pretence, and exposed them relentlessly for what they were. His words fell like whip-lashes: and humanly speaking, they finally sealed His doom. The chief priests and rulers could not allow a public attack of this kind to pass: these caustic words would be ringing through the land within a few days, and their authority would be shaken to its foundations, if not gone for ever. These words made the cross inevitable and immediate: but Jesus uttered them because they were the truth. Very shortly afterwards He bore witness before Pilate, "For this cause came I into the world, that I should bear witness unto the truth. Every one that is of the truth heareth my voice." That is the essential character of His Kingdom and His Gospel. And declaration of the truth often includes and necessitates exposure of deception and falsehood.

Thus Jesus walked the road to the cross; a walk of faith and obedience—just such as we, His disciples, are called to walk. His having set out upon that road did not mean submitting to an impetus which would carry Him inevitably to the appointed end. Every step had to be taken deliberately, of His own steadfast volition; at each cross-road the determined purpose manifest thus far had to be re-affirmed and wrought out. That is the principle and the practice of faith.

In our identification with Him in the way of the cross, the same principle and practice apply. We too are called upon to set our feet on that road—and to tread it resolutely, in daily fellowship with the Lord and embracing of His will. "If any man will come after me," said Jesus, "let him deny himself, and take up His cross *daily*, and follow me . . ." It is a walk of faith; a walking with the Lord. Only so can we be His true disciples.

9

Clash with Authority

NOTHING in our human experience is easier than to drift with the tide: nothing is more difficult than to be "odd man out." This tendency of human nature presented our Lord with one of the first great testings of His public ministry. To win substantial support for His Messianic ministry and message, He would need to gain the goodwill of the priests and leaders of the nation. The common people might gather round Him in multitudes, and eagerly assent to His words: but the whim of the populace was notoriously capricious. If He were to be recognised and received as Messiah, it must be by the Sanhedrin and the group of influential men who formed and controlled it. But these people were, for the most part, cynical, self-seeking materialists, usurpers of religious office for personal gain; men who in character and outlook and daily deeds denied and defied the Law they were pledged to uphold. It is not surprising, therefore, that one of the first of His public acts in Jerusalem brought Jesus into direct conflict with these men. It was the beginning of a clash with authority which developed into an open breach, and precipitated the inevitable issue of their submission to His claims or their accomplishing His death. There could be no alternative. And He knew from the beginning which of these two possible courses they would follow. Already His feet were on that road to the cross.

During His first visit to Jerusalem as a boy of twelve, Jesus had tarried in the temple after Joseph and Mary had set off with their neighbours and friends for Nazareth, thinking that He was in the company; and to their remonstrance when at length they found Him, the lad replied, "Wist ye not that I must be about my Father's affairs"—or, "in my Father's House," according to the R.V. rendering. The worship and service of God, in the appointed sacrifices and ritual of the temple, thrilled His whole being. But in subsequent visits He could not fail to see much to disturb and distress Him. How soon had He been outraged in spirit by the realisation of the cynical and self-seeking commercialisation of the very worship of the sanctuary, by the hierarchy and priesthood? We may be sure that, long before His public ministry began, His soul burned with indignation at the lust for gain rife in the very precincts of the House of God, in the crafty transactions of the money-changers and the unscrupulous profiteering in the sale of animals for sacrifice. These things were a disgrace to the temple and a degradation of the Name of the One who there should be supremely honoured and adored.

At the very beginning of His ministry, therefore, in dissociation of Himself from this disgraceful perversion of the worship of Jehovah, and in denunciation of those who perpetrated it, He purged the temple, overturning the tables of the money-changers and casting out those who were selling beasts. His burning words of scornful rebuke matched the fervour of His action: "Take these things hence; make not my Father's House an House of merchandise!" In this action He fulfilled—as His disciples recognised—the prophetic intimation of the psalmist, "The zeal of Thine House hath eaten me up" (Ps. 69: 9; John 2: 17). The die was cast; the breach was immediate and irrevocable: henceforth the priests and rulers were His sworn enemies. They could not endure this exposure of their falsehood; this assault upon their authority; this threat to their means of gain. They would show Him that He could not attack them with impunity! Nor could He refrain from further denunciation of these and kindred evils. His clash with the "powers that be" must persist, to its fateful issue. The Messiah had not come, however, to establish His Kingdom by diplomacy and compromise: He had come to redeem—and could only do so by means of a cross.

It is characteristic of religious decadence, that great emphasis is placed upon the incidentals and trappings of outward forms and ceremonies, in order—consciously or otherwise—to deflect attention from the lack of true spiritual worship and inward reality. No one was more meticulous in the niceties of such conventional nonsense, than these Sadducees and Pharisees. They had, in their professed zeal, added to the Law of God a multitude of petty rules and regulations governing all aspects of life, until these had become a burden grievous to be borne; but the enforcement of them enhanced their prestige and authority. Under the pretence of honouring God, they had imposed their own yoke upon the people.

Jesus exposed this sterile code for what it was. In defying their man-made rules, He unmasked their hypocritical folly and brought the people back to the simplicities of true spiritual faith and worship. Thus, when they challenged Him because His disciples plucked and ate ears of corn on the Sabbath, alleging that "Thy disciples do that which is not lawful to do upon the Sabbath day," He reminded them how David and his followers had, uncondemned, entered the House of God and eaten the shewbread, which it was not lawful for any but the priests to eat. To this weighty precedent, our Lord added the stinging comment, "If ye had known what this meaneth, 'I will have mercy, and not sacrifice,' ye would not have condemned the guiltless." Not only did He vindicate the disciples—and His own tacit consent to their act—but He "turned the tables" by indicting these self-righteous critics (Matt. 12: 1–7). Again, when confronted with sick and afflicted folk, He healed them—even on the Sabbath day; and to the outraged, protesting priests He averred that such deeds were the very works of God; that, in the restoration of His children to health and peace and joy, and putting in their mouths songs of thanksgiving, God was glorified, rather than by the observance of their pettifogging regulations (Matt. 12: 9–14; Luke 13: 10–17). For this outspoken scorn of their barren and lifeless legalism, they hated Him; not only because He publicly exposed their folly, but also because He undermined their authority over the people. Their anger so blinded them, that the very miracles which authenticated His Messianic claims, provoked them to plot together "how they might destroy Him" (Matt. 12: 14). This is the first mention of their consulting together to plan His death: from that time on, their hostility was relentless and unremitting—and directed always to that end. It was, indeed, open warfare. And Jesus met them on that ground, denouncing their hypocrisy and sinister schemings.

They went so far as to allege that His casting out of devils was by the power of Beelzebub: but Jesus, with a light touch, scattered that suggestion to the winds, by pointing out that a house divided against itself cannot stand. The folly of the allegation that He cast out Satan by Satan recoiled upon themselves—and underlined the only alternative explanation, that His casting out of devils was by the Spirit of God (Matt. 12: 28). Then the Lord thrust home the stern warning, that to attribute the acts of the Spirit of God to Beelzebub, was to commit a blasphemy for which there could be no forgiveness (v. 32). Thus did He once again not only rout them, but also reproached them before the people. This discomfiture, to men accustomed to obsequious esteem, was extremely galling; and it inflamed their hatred of Him. Never learning from their experience, however, they returned yet again to the attack, by demanding a sign from Him (Matt. 12: 38). He answered that He would give them none, save the sign of the prophet Jonah. "For as Jonas was three days and three nights in the whale's belly, so shall the Son of Man be three days and three nights in the heart of the earth" (v. 40). How significant was that! The supreme sign of His Messiahship was—the very cross to which they would drive Him! In His combat with them, He was fully aware of the outcome; He consciously and deliberately was walking that road to the cross. They might regard it as a triumph of their schemings, but it would rather be the accomplishing of His sovereign purpose as the Messiah of Israel and the Saviour of the world.

Unable to trap Him in His words or to find a single fault in His deeds, these evil men again sought to wound Him through His disciples. "Why," they asked, "do Thy disciples transgress the tradition of the elders? for they wash not their hands when they eat bread" (Matt. 15: 2). With characteristic riposte He replied, "Why do *ye* transgress the commandment of God by your tradition . . ." and went on to give devastating examples. The sting lay in the condemnation of their cherished "tradition" when examined in the light of the commandment of God. The regulations they imposed were not only burdensome, but utterly inimical to both the spirit and the letter of the Law. They were, indeed, nullifying the Law by their unwarranted additions thereto—"This people draweth nigh unto me with their mouth, and honoureth me with their lips; but their heart is far from me" (v. 8). The effect of this upon His critics was so startling that the disciples came to Jesus, and said, afterwards apprehensively, "Knowest Thou that the Pharisees were offended, after they heard this saying?" (v. 12). His reply was forthright: "Let them alone: they be blind leaders of the blind . . ." (v. 14).

All this had cumulative effect, in hardening their hostility, and uniting even the incompatible Pharisees and Sadducees in a combined effort to silence Him. They whispered together angrily in their chagrin, planning a master-move which would bring about His downfall. They sought out the most subtle minds among them, to devise questions which would set a snare for Him, so that however He answered He could not avoid angering the people. One suggestion after another was considered and tried, until at last a question was devised which, answered yea or nay, would equally inflame the populace. With jubilation they came in strength to Him, at a time when there was a great multitude around to hear, and to witness His confusion; and in ringing tones they asked the question which they thought would disgrace Him for ever—"Should we pay taxes to Cæsar, or not?" If He said "No," they would report Him to the Roman authorities for inciting the mob to rebellion; if He said "Yes," the people would break out in uproar—and they could leave the infuriated rabble to deal with Him! Here, they thought, was a dilemma which even He could not evade or escape.

A hush fell upon the multitude: all were intent upon hearing His reply. This was a matter which stirred every Jewish soul to its depths. It wasn't the fact of having to pay taxes that they resented so fiercely, but the servitude it expressed. What had Jesus of Nazareth to say about it? Instead of showing any consternation at the question, however, He calmly replied, "Show me a penny." Then, one being produced, He asked, "Whose is this image and superscription?" To which they answered in one word, "Cæsar's." Then, "Render therefore unto Cæsar the things which are Cæsar's; and unto God, the things that are God's." The hush which held the crowd in its grip was sustained: all realised that they had been confronted with a challenge which condemned them, and with a standard of faith and devotion to God from which they fell short. The hostile questioners were confounded and awed by the unearthly wisdom of His reply, which not only frustrated their evil intentions, but made them again look foolish. They "marvelled," says Matthew: and they slunk away speechless (22: 22). Such men are not subdued, however, by any manifestation of wisdom and authority which challenge their own; so instead of acknowledging that this was an answer worthy of the Christ, they plotted the more intently to put Him to death.

In that last week of His earthly life, between the triumphal entry into Jerusalem and His crucifixion, Jesus was in almost constant conflict with these adversaries. The climax had been reached; the final battle had been joined; they determined that, somehow, they would trap and overcome Him. The Lord had for the second time cleansed the temple: repeating at the close of His ministry the dramatic protest and purification with which He had begun His Messianic mission. This time He added the sterner denunciation, that they were transforming the temple into a den of thieves. Then He publicly declared them to be unworthy of the offices they held; in a series of most solemn "woes" He denounced them, and in a group of parables pronounced the judgment of God upon them (Matt. 21: 18–46). Like a barren fig tree, having the "leaves" of outward profession without the fruit which should accompany such profession, the blight of God would come upon them. Like the unworthy and rebellious tenants who refused to render to the householder the fruits of his vineyard, but maltreated his servants and killed his son, they should be punished with sore judgment. They would not heed this final warning, however, but hardened their hearts still further: they plotted with a traitor, and indicted Him on a trumped-up charge before the Roman Governor whom they would otherwise have scorned to recognise as exercising authority over them. Thus the clash with the religious leaders of His day led Jesus to the cross.

Countless of His disciples also have, since that day and until our own, walked that road, for His sake, and in fellowship with Him. For, despite the clear lessons and warnings of this record in the Word, the self-same conditions have prevailed in the Church again and again, as in the Israel of our Lord's day. There have ever been—and still are—those only too ready to regard religion as a means of their own advancement and enrichment. All too often the sacred vocation of the Christian ministry has been violated by a spirit of professionalism, and even of sordid careerism. The inevitable result is the substitution of ritualism for spiritual reality; the doctrine of salvation by works, with the attendant evils of an arid legalism, in place of a humble walk with God by faith and in obedience to His Word. Alas, it is so easy to drift with the tide; so difficult to withstand prevalent customs and practices. But Luther did; Wesley did; the Non-jurors did—and countless unnamed heroes of faith who are worthy to rank with those whose stories are recorded in Hebrews 11.

And we? Are we content with conditions in our day—in our Church; among the religious leaders of our nation? Is there not today a Laodicean lifelessness in many churches; a formality and barren ritualism—austere or elaborate—which tragically misrepresents the good tidings of great joy which the Church should be proclaiming, and the "life more abundant" it should be manifesting? Are we, perhaps, carried by the tide; or ought we to take our stand against it? Be sure of this: that any such attitude or act would mean the way of the cross, for all who follow it, as certainly as it did for the File-leader of our faith.

10

Perils of Popularity

IT might seem self-contradictory to speak of the perils of popularity, in relation to the Lord Jesus, immediately after condemning the blind and criminal folly of the priests and pharisees in rejecting Him as their Messiah. For was not the acclaim of the people just such recognition of Him as the leaders of the nation refused to render? Plausible as this reasoning might appear, however, it is false: for the plaudits of the crowd were animated by a spirit as self-seeking as that of the pharisees; this popular acclaim was as far from submission to His word and will, as was the hostility of our Lord's open enemies. The two attitudes were opposite sides of the one coin of self-centred reaction to the ministry of the Messiah.

History abounds in illustrations of the fickleness of the mob. There was nothing extraordinary in the change of cry, within a few days, from "Hosannah to the Son of David" to "Crucify Him!" Jesus certainly was not deceived by their ebullient enthusiasm at any time during His ministry: He "did not commit Himself unto them," John declares regarding the fervour which attended His early days in Galilee, "because He knew all men" (John 2: 24). But He did not on that account withdraw from them; still less did He spurn them. He looked upon them with compassion, as sheep without a shepherd: He longed to reveal to them God as He really is, and to make them understand the mission of grace on which He had sent His only-begotten Son. But like the scribes and pharisees, they had their own ideas concerning the Messiah, and were blind and deaf to all else. When His miracles encouraged them to believe that Jesus was indeed the Christ, they leaped to their own conclusions and greeted Him *as the Messiah they desired*, rather than the Messiah He was. In their clamorous acclaim of Him there lay greater danger, possibly, than in the cold enmity of the supercilious ruling clique. For while it would inevitably lead to the same end—a Roman cross—it might also establish for all time wrong conceptions of the true character of His claims and His Kingdom.

Jesus therefore avoided the popularity of the people even more assiduously than he denounced the errors and ambitions of the priests. And this was the harder task of the two. It would have been easy, had He chosen to avoid the people, to withdraw with His few intimate friends and disciples, to instruct and equip them in private for future service. But He had come to show forth the heart of the Father, who "so loved *the world* that He gave His only begotten Son . . ." He Himself looked upon the people with loving compassion. He delighted in proclaiming to them the good tidings of the Kingdom; He moved among them, performing acts of healing and mercy. He avoided their misdirected enthusiasm while not—emphatically not—avoiding them. In that, He exemplified for this entire dispensation of grace, His dealings with the frailties and follies of men.

So it is that we see Jesus, in the Gospel narratives, in the midst of great multitudes—on the highway, in the temple, out in the fields, on a mountain-side, in their homes: speaking as never man spake, and performing works of mercy and grace which showed forth the loving-kindness as well as the power of the Almighty. In all the varied circumstances and scenes of life; on all occasions and in all needs, we behold Him bringing to the people the word of divine revelation and the invitation of heavenly grace.

The crowds, however, went bent upon the Utopia of their dreams, which they fondly imagined the Messiah would initiate. And when His miracles attested Jesus to be the Messiah, their feverish anticipations were given free rein. Excitement reached its climax after the feeding of the five thousand. This could be nothing but the realisation of their wildest hopes: the provision of life's necessities without toil, by miracle! Who would not wish for such a king! So "they would come and take Him by force, to make Him king" (John 6: 15); but Jesus forestalled them, by departing again into a mountain alone.

Mankind has ever yearned for such a king as these Jews desired, and will follow any leader or creed giving promise of material benefits. That constitutes the appeal of Communism in our day, among the less privileged people of the world. But Jesus had not come to satisfy the mundane desires of man's physical being: while He showed plainly His concern for human welfare, He declared equally plainly that His Kingdom was not of this world—as He said later to Pilate. He had come to establish the Kingdom of God in the hearts of redeemed men; to manifest the reign of righteousness and the rule of God's Anointed. Once His sovereignty was thus established, it would reach out to the whole range of human concerns: the needs of the body, and the manifestation of righteousness and equity in all the affairs of men, would come within the scope of His rule.

Their error lay in confusing cause and effect; in a totally wrong sense of values: in making a by-product of His reign to occupy first place in all their thoughts and hopes concerning His Kingdom. Therefore He withdrew; and when they came to Him again later, still agog with materialistic anticipations, He sternly rebuked them. "Ye seek me," He said, "because ye did eat of the loaves and were filled," and He went on to show the difference between His conceptions of the Kingdom, and theirs. "Labour not for the meat which perisheth, but for that meat which shall endure unto everlasting life, which the Son of Man shall give unto you . . . ." And as He proceeded to explain the true nature of that "bread"—the provision He had come to make for their deepest needs—not only did their ardour cool, but even "many of His disciples went back, and walked no more with Him." The peril of popularity was thus resolutely put aside, and left Him still walking steadily onward along the road to the cross.

Once more, however, the fickle crowds—ever optimistic that their cherished dreams would come true—thought to make Him an earthly king; and this time He seemed not only to encourage them, but to be on the point of claiming the throne of David. Entering Jerusalem as a prophet of old had predicted, riding on an ass, He made no attempt to silence their excited shouts, "Hosannah to the Son of David . . . Blessed be the king that cometh in the Name of the Lord!" Instead of setting up the standard of rebellion against Rome, however; instead of summoning the warriors of the nation or the hosts of heaven to eject the hated Gentile; instead of promising them national greatness and unprecedented prosperity, He went His way quietly to the temple, and there—did nothing but look around, with flashing and scornful eye, upon its scene of merchandise and desecration.

Matthew's account reads as if Jesus cleansed the temple that same day; the purpose of the Evangelist is to show the closest connection between the triumphal entry, and all that it signified, and the purging of the temple: to emphasise that *this* was His kingly work. The other Evangelists indicate, however, that after His searching glance around the temple, He went out to Bethany again for the night, and next morning returned to overthrow the tables of the money-changers and drive out those who sold beasts. All the Gospel writers make clear that this was His regal act, the exercise of His authority as Messiah the King—postponed from the night before, probably, because of the effect it might then have had upon the excited crowd, which was ready for any riotous and irresponsible demonstration. By this cleansing of the temple a second time, however, He indicated once more the true character of His Messianic ministry and reign. It related, not to the realm of nationalistic politics and material matters, but to His Father's House; to the worship and service of God; to relationship with the Most High—the doing of His will and observing of His word.

The people were disappointed, and the rulers incensed: and these usually disparate groups now joined hands in enmity against Him. There is no hatred more bitter than that of people disappointed of high hopes, no matter how irrational those hopes may have been. So it was that the lips which had cried "Hosannah" were ready soon to shout, "Crucify Him!" Jesus was fully aware that He was on the road to the cross, even amid the Messianic greetings of His triumphal ride into Jerusalem.

Now, we are considering the road to the cross, not merely to observe Jesus as a historical figure steadfastly pursuing His way thereon, but in order to keep Him company on that road, insofar as we may. For there is a counterpart in our day of that road, and He would have us to walk it as His disciples. "He that taketh not his cross, and followeth after me," Jesus said, "is not worthy of me" (Matt. 10: 38). Still more plainly, "Whosoever doth not bear his cross, and come after me, cannot be my disciple" (Luke 14: 27). Yet, strangely, we find that the Church has seemingly ignored the lessons of these Gospel narratives, and neglected the explicit commands and warnings of the Lord.

The perils of popularity, so clearly indicated and so resolutely avoided by Jesus, have beset His followers through all succeeding generations; and they have all too often succumbed to the subtle temptations, rather than resisting them. Indeed, the two complementary evils of religious arrogance and popular favour, which Jesus combated and overcame, have been welcomed and embraced, so that the very forces and factors which combined to crucify the Lord have been adopted by and absorbed into the Church. How amazing it is, in the light of the Gospel records, that in the Name of Jesus the crucified, a religious institutionalism should have been allowed to flourish within the Church, the very counterpart of that which rejected the Lord. It was in times of decline and decadence that religious arrogance reared its head, in the creation of popes and prelates, "princes" and priests of the Church, when its Founder had most solemnly declared—under the very shadow of the cross—"Be not ye called Rabbi: for one is your Master, even Christ; and all ye are brethren. And call no man your father upon the earth; for one is your Father, which is in heaven. Neither be ye called masters, for one is your Master, even Christ. But he that is greatest among you shall be your servant" (Matt. 23: 8–11). And again, "The kings of the Gentiles exercise lordship over them; and they that exercise authority upon them are called benefactors. But ye shall not be so: but he that is greatest among you, let him be as the younger; and he that is chief, as he that doth serve. For . . . I am among you as He that serveth" (Luke 22: 25–27). These principles have ever been re-asserted in times of Reformation and Revival, and the twin yokes of ecclesiastical arrogance and of *vox populi* have been thrown off. Today, it would seem that we are in greater peril than at any time since Luther raised his voice against the blasphemies of Rome: for under the persuasive plea of Christian unity those characteristics of hierarchical authority and popular favour tend to be increasingly exalted, and the

63

spiritual heritage and values of the New Testament, of the Reformation and times of Revival, submerged.

The road to the cross was a lonely road for the Lord: maybe it will become increasingly so as the age draws toward its close, for all who would keep Him company as His true followers.

Viewed from a Mountain

MOUNTAINS occupy a prominent rôle in the Bible. They are strategic meeting places of God and man. On a mountain, Abraham was ready to offer Isaac as a sacrifice, in obedience to God's command; deeply perplexed and distressed, doubtless, but confident that God would raise the lad from the dead, since He had promised that in this son the purpose of blessing for all nations of the earth should be realised. There, on the mount, assuredly, Abraham had that vision and that understanding of a future sacrifice, of which our Lord spoke when He said, "Abraham rejoiced to see my day; and he saw it, and was glad" (John 8: 56). Abraham knew that measure of fellowship with the Lord along the road that led to the cross.

On a mountain, later, the Law was given: the Law which, violated, condemns; but also the Law which, in grace, provided the place of pardon through repentance and sacrifice. Moses, who received that Law from the very hands of God upon Sinai's flaming summit, was himself judged by it, and forbidden to enter the land of promise; yet from another mountain he was granted a glimpse of the land in its expanse and beauty.

A mountain top is unexampled as a place of vision, and on a mount the Lord Jesus surveyed the last stretch of the road before Him, leading so soon to that other mount, called Calvary. On a mountain He had given His first great sermon, the "Manifesto of the Kingdom," as Dr. Campbell Morgan used to describe it. On a mountain He oft-times withdrew to commune with His Father; from a mountain He saw the disciples toiling in rowing, and went to their aid, walking upon the water. Now it was upon a mountain that the mysterious experience which we know as the Transfiguration occurred.

What precisely happened when our Lord "was transfigured before them"—that is, Peter and James and John? There are two explanations which are widely held among Evangelical Bible students. One, popularised by Dr. Campbell Morgan, is that Jesus there experienced momentarily, as man, that seal upon His perfect obedience and sinless humanity, which Adam would have gained had he remained unfallen. In a word, it was a brief manifestation of the heavenly glory with which the earthly body of Adam would have been invested had he resisted temptation, remained without sin, and wholly loved and obeyed the Lord God.

Although Adam was created in the image and likeness of God, his body was earthy and conditioned for earthly existence; it would have needed—according to this point of view—to be changed (as our redeemed bodies will be at the resurrection) for its eternal and heavenly estate. Adam sinned; and in sinning, forfeited that transfiguration of his body which he might have known. Our Lord Jesus, however, the second Adam, was holy, harmless, undefiled, separate from sinners; and by His perfect holiness and obedience, He merited as man that glorification of His human frame which Adam forfeited: and on the mount He received the attestation of His achieving that goal. Thus, according to this view, He gained not only for Himself but also for all who are "in Christ," the glorification of our human personality and frame: "for as in Adam all die, so in Christ shall all be . . . changed, in a moment, in the twinkling of an eye, at the last trump . . ." (1 Cor. 15: 22, 52, 53).

The traditional interpretation of the great event on the mount, however, is that the Transfiguration was, not our Lord's glorification as perfect man, but a momentary outshining of His eternal glory as the Son of God. He had laid aside the visible manifestation of His glory when He became Son of Man: but He had not ceased to be the Son of God. He made Himself of no reputation, and took upon Him the form of a servant; nevertheless He was still essentially the Lord of glory. Yet, being found in fashion as a man, He humbled Himself still further, and was about to submit to the indescribable shame and suffering of the death of the cross.

He faced that ordeal in all the weakness of His true, most

sensitive, humanity; and as a man He shrank from it. "Now is my soul troubled; and what shall I say? Father, save me from this hour; but for this cause came I unto this hour. Father, glorify Thy name" (John 12: 27, 28). Those were not only His words during the days of tension immediately preceding His arrest and crucifixion, but doubtless His repeated prayer on the road to the cross.

Now on the mount, we are told that He faced this most solemn issue: there appeared Moses and Elijah, talking with Him "of His decease which He should accomplish at Jerusalem." There was manifestly a twofold purpose in the Transfiguration: to strengthen our Lord Himself, as man, for the truly terrible ordeal before Him; and to instruct the disciples concerning His Person and purpose. It is clear that the disciples had no part in the discussion between the Lord, Moses and Elijah: so that "conference" was primarily to fortify Him, rather than to instruct them. Equally, the very fact that the Lord had taken them there, is evidence enough that He nevertheless had something to teach them from this experience.

As a man, Jesus was about to endure, not only the agonies summed up in the term, His Passion, but supremely that experience of dereliction of which we have only the dimmest comprehension, out of which He would utter that terrible cry, "My God, my God, why hast Thou forsaken me?" His consciousness of oneness with the Father had inspired all His life and ministry: but that consciousness was to depart from Him, in that dread hour upon the tree, as He was "made to be sin for us"; the face of the Father would of necessity be turned from the sin-bearer. But in that moment He would render the supreme act of obedience and filial love; and instead of being forsaken, would accomplish the eternal purpose of God in the reconciliation of sinful man unto Himself.

As the seal of God upon His obedience as Son of Man, and as confirmation of the Father's good pleasure, therefore, "He received from God the Father honour and glory, when there came such a voice to Him from the excellent glory, This is my beloved Son, in whom I am well pleased" (2 Peter 1: 17). He who was seemingly to be abandoned by God now had, to strengthen His faith and resolution, this brief experience of the investiture of His human body with that glory which He had voluntarily laid aside. What the three privileged disciples saw was most assuredly an outshining of His eternal glory; for "we were eye-witnesses of His majesty," Peter testifies—and that word *majesty* relates to His Deity. The One to be despised and rejected of men, and seemingly forsaken of God, was nevertheless the Son of God, in whom the Father delighted —and never more so than in that hour of apparent estrangement.

Now the word used to describe the "decease" which He was to accomplish in Jerusalem, is arresting: it is *exodus*. He was not merely to die; but in dying was to effect deliverance for those held captive by sin and death. A greater Moses, He was to lead His people out of the bondage of the world, the flesh and the devil, into the glorious liberty of the sons of God. No wonder Moses was one of the two sent to commune with and strengthen Him. Henceforward, fortified by this experience, He steadfastly "for the joy that was set before Him endured the cross, despising the shame"—the joy of "bringing many sons unto glory" (Heb. 2: 10; 12: 2).

The transfiguration of His body was a foretaste of His exaltation as Man; it was an earnest of that glorification as the Redeemer and Head of the new creation, which should follow the Passion of the cross; the assurance of His future triumph as the Man and Mediator and great High Priest in the throne. It was a pledge that the bodies of those He was about to redeem would be glorified; for as man He was representative of the race and Saviour of all who put their trust in Him. Through His death—rather than His life: though the two are essentially united—He secured their future participation in His glory; for "whom He justified, them He also glorified." But the condition is, the fellowship of His sufferings—"If so be that we suffer with Him, that we might be glorified together . . ." (Rom. 8: 30, 17).

But more: Peter relates the Transfiguration to the "*power* and *coming* of our Lord Jesus Christ . . ." (v. 16). The first of these two words relates to His almighty resources as God; and the second, to His ultimate triumph in His Second Advent. The apostle had declared, a few verses earlier, that "His (God's) divine power hath given us all things that pertain unto life and godliness" (v. 3). The word *dunamis* manifestly expresses the infinite resources of the omnipotent God; and that is the word here applied to Christ. And "coming" is used exclusively of His Advent as King of kings and Lord of lords—the consummation of His purposes in His triumphant appearing, when His Church shall be complete, and presented unto Him as a Bride adorned for her marriage.

The Transfiguration, then, was the manifestation of His Deity, and a prophecy of His eventual appearing in glory. It was the attestation of God that "He who shall come will come, and will not tarry." The road to the cross does not end at Calvary, but proceeds beyond—unto His Coming.

Yet again, the Transfiguration was the divine confirmation of the Old Testament prophecies concerning the Messiah: the attestation that Jesus was indeed the One long predicted. He was the prophet raised up like unto Moses; the Son of David explicitly promised; the Servant whom Isaiah foretold, who was yet the Lamb led to the slaughter. We have, through the Transfiguration, Peter declares, "a more sure word of prophecy" (v. 19); a word not only vindicated in its explicit fulfilment, but still pointing onward to a further purpose of God yet to be outwrought. We can trust it absolutely, for in Jesus it is doubly attested: it is "more sure" to us even than to the prophets and seers who spoke it and anticipated its fulfilment.

While the outshining of His glory was thus a means of grace and strength to Jesus in the self-imposed limitations of His manhood, it was also deeply instructive to the disciples. They had realised that He was quite different from any other man; they believed unquestioningly that He was the Messiah: but only by revelation from the Father could they know that He was the very Son of God. Even after Peter's confession at Cæsarea Philippi, they did not fully apprehend what this really meant: that He was truly the eternal Son of the Father, God incarnate, the Second Person of the Trinity. How could they, since they had no conception of the Trinity; of God in three Persons? That illumination could come only from above; and it could not be grasped all at once. But on the mount they realised that He was no mere man: not even the greatest of men. Something of the sublime truth must have dawned upon them, not only from what they beheld of the effulgence of the divine glory in Jesus, but also from the words from heaven concerning Him: "This is my beloved Son . . ."

We speak of the road to the cross, then, never as leading to that stark event as an end, but rather as a means—an inevitable means—to a glorious end, even the redemption of mankind. In the fulfilling of the purposes of God through that plan of redemption, the apostles had a great part to play; and their education and illumination concerning Jesus of Nazareth was vital. What it meant to Peter is clear from these glowing words of his, written long afterwards, in his second epistle. To him, the Transfiguration was a supreme event, setting the seal of God upon the Person and ministry of the Lord, and upon all the prophetic Scriptures concerning Him. And central to that remarkable event, was the discussion of His "decease."

Withdrawn for a while from the turmoil and travail of the road to the cross, He yet surveyed it calmly from the lofty height of the mountain. Then, strengthened by the token and word of the Father's good pleasure, He confirmed His resolve to pursue His walk along that road. And so, with the three wondering disciples, He descended from the mountain, to the clamour and challenge of the valley—where not only a tormented boy and distressed father awaited Him, but adversaries determined upon His death—little realising that thereby He would redeem the world.

12

A Pause at Bethany

JESUS valued human companionship very highly. His first act on commencing His public ministry was to call the group of disciples to be His *companions in the way*. Of course, He chose them to be the future leaders of His Church; from the first He was training them for their post-pentecostal responsibilities as His apostles. Nevertheless, we lose much of the import of the Gospel story if we subdue its note of human friendship between the Lord and the Eleven—for we must exclude Judas, even as he excluded himself from truly intimate relationship with the Lord, despite the privilege he had of close contact with the Son of God incarnate.

Our Lord chose this band of men, Mark tells us, "*that they should be with Him,* and that He might send them forth to preach . . .*" It is impossible to draw any sharp distinction between the human friendship and the Messianic purposes of Jesus toward the Eleven: the two are intertwined; yet in pursuing His way and fulfilling His purposes as the Messiah, He was nevertheless truly human, and repeatedly we have evidence of His gratitude for their companionship, and His longing for even closer friendship and more intimate understanding on their part than they were then able to give. It is highly important to realise this, for the relationship of the Lord with the Eleven most vividly illustrates for us the fellowship into which He invites all His disciples. He is the Man Christ Jesus: and although we worship Him as our Lord and our God, nevertheless He came to redeem men in order to satisfy the longing of God for true fellowship. The heavenly host render Him unceasing and unalloyed worship: but the adoration of angels and archangels, cherubim and seraphim could not meet that need of the divine heart for *fellowship*; that is why man was created, in His own image and likeness, capable of rendering it—and despite the fall, capable still of doing so, when redeemed and regenerate. It is not enough, then, that we should worship God: above and beyond our worship, He desires our love, our fellowship—yes, our *friendship*. "I have called you friends," said Jesus to the Eleven, on the very eve of His cross; and He spoke that word not only to them, but to all who will hear His voice and respond to His grace.

The friendship of Jesus was not limited to the Eleven: we read of others, and especially some women, who shared that privilege with the apostles. Certainly we must put the family at Bethany in that category. When Lazarus was taken ill, his sisters did not hesitate to send to Jesus the simple message, "He whom Thou lovest is sick." From that brief message there ensued the most notable and most momentous miracle of our Lord's entire ministry.

Never did Jesus act more perplexingly, to our human way of thinking, than when He deliberately lingered "beyond Jordan" despite the implicit appeal of that message. His delay pierced the two sisters, Martha and Mary, to the heart: both said to Him, with grieved reproach, when at length He arrived at Bethany, four days after their brother's death, "If Thou hadst been here, he would not have died." They had doubtless said this to one another, concerning Jesus, again and again; and naturally enough they used identical words in expressing to the Lord what had been uppermost in their minds these four long, dark days. But Jesus had allowed the seeming tragedy "for the glory of God"—as He had already explained to the Twelve. He had vitally important lessons to teach them—and all mankind—through this apparent disaster. At the tomb, He uttered the most comforting assurance ever given to men concerning death and the mystery of the grave: golden words, cherished by all the saints in all the ages since; robbing death of its sting and the grave of its victory. "I am the resurrection and the life: he that believeth in me, though he were dead, yet shall he live. And whosoever liveth and believeth in me shall never die . . ." Then with commanding voice He called to the occupant of the tomb, "Lazarus, come forth!"—and the man, bound in grave-clothes, came forth.

With the raising of one not only dead but buried for four days, Jesus demonstrated His Lordship of life and authority over death; this was the final, ultimate sign and seal of His Messiahship, the supreme evidence of divine authority and power. Even the sceptical Sadducees could not dispute that an amazing miracle had been wrought; but instead of submitting to its implications, they determined the more resolutely to put Him to death (John 11: 53). For what reason? "If we let Him thus alone, all men will believe on Him, and the Romans shall come and take away both *our place* and nation." Despite irrefutable evidence that Jesus was the Messiah, they plotted His death for fear that *their place* might be in jeopardy! "His (Christ's) spiritual teaching was cutting at the very root of their whole being," observes the late Dean Plumptre, in *Ellicott's Commentary*: "If all the people believed on Him . . . the Romans would take away both their position, and with it the rank which they still claimed . . ." And they thought more of these, than they did of the divine purposes in the coming of Messiah! Such were the religious leaders of Israel, the chosen people of God.

Knowing their intention, Jesus again withdrew for a short while, until six days before the Passover. Then He returned to Bethany, where a "supper" was prepared for Him, doubtless in gratitude for the raising of Lazarus. During the meal, Mary brought her costly gift of spikenard, for the anointing of His head and feet: and the fragrance of it not only filled the house, but lingers yet, wherever this story is read or told. This was one of the most beautiful and moving incidents in the whole Gospel story: and it shines the brighter against the dark background of the hostility and evil purposes of the chief priests and rulers. This act of loving devotion is an inspiration and example to all who owe the Lord a debt of gratitude we can never hope to repay, but can nevertheless express in a manner which is to Him as ointment poured forth.

There are several problems, of a textual and chronological character, that must be briefly considered, in relation to this eventful occasion. The story is told by Matthew, Mark and John; and the first two Evangelists seem to imply that the supper was held toward the end of the last week in our Lord's earthly life, for they proceed immediately to tell of the departure of Judas to the chief priests, to covenant with them concerning the betrayal of the Lord. The purpose of the writers

73

is to emphasise the close connection between Mary's gift and the final decision of Judas to play the traitor: this lavish display of devotion to Jesus—with its hint of impending death—was the "last straw" which impelled him to his foul deed. John, more meticulous in his chronology, says specifically that the supper was held on the eve of our Lord's triumphal entry into Jerusalem—that is, after the Sabbath had ended, officially, which it did at 6 p.m. It was customary to have a meal thus after the Sabbath, and this festive occasion could be held on no more fitting day.

Another problem which arises from a comparison of the records in all three Gospels is, Where was the supper held? Matthew and Mark state that it was in the house of Simon the leper—presumably an erstwhile leper, whom Jesus had cleansed. We know nothing more about him, though some expositors suggest that he might have been the father of Lazarus, Martha and Mary; or Martha's husband; or a friendly neighbour. The expression used by John, that "Lazarus was one of them that sat at table with Him," seems to imply that Lazarus also, like Jesus, was a guest; but on the other hand, Martha and Mary behaved as if they were at home—and if not literally so, they were manifestly as much "at home" in this household as Mary, the mother of Jesus, was in the home at Cana where He performed His first miracle—when she was concerned about the shortage of wine, spoke to Jesus about it, and then had a word in the ear of the servants, "Whatsoever He saith unto you, do it!"

Matthew and Mark do not mention Mary of Bethany by name: John alone identifies her as the one who wrought this "good work" upon the Lord. Luke does not record the event at all: but he tells of the earlier incident in the house of Simon the pharisee, when a woman who was a sinner came in and washed the feet of Jesus with her tears, and anointed His head and feet with ointment (Luke 7: 36–50). Some critics argue that this was one and the same occasion as that which we are considering, transposed in time and altered in details by the Evangelist, for literary reasons: but the differences are considerable, and the two events manifestly distinct. Equally unsatisfactory is the assumption of Archbishop William Temple—adopting the teaching of the Roman Church—that Mary was the woman on both occasions, repeating in Bethany her earlier act of devotion and gratitude for being forgiven and restored. This is as unwarranted by the facts in Scripture, and as foreign to the spirit of the narrative, as the other suggestion. That Mary of Bethany was "a woman in the city, a sinner," is utterly incredible. She may possibly have heard of that earlier event, however, and been inspired by it to her own expression of loving gratitude to the Lord: but that is the only connection between the two incidents we are warranted in inferring from the Scriptures.

The supper was proceeding happily when Mary quietly arose and, fetching the flask of precious nard, crushed it, and anointed the head and feet of the Lord. Immediately there was silence, and all eyes were fastened on Mary. Then a gruff murmuring, and the scornful expostulation of Judas, "To what purpose is this waste?" The rest of the apostles joined in, and re-echoed his further carping query, "Why was not this ointment sold for three hundred pence, and given to the poor?" Now, that estimate of Judas concerning the value of the ointment was probably correct; and three hundred *denarii* was indeed a goodly sum—practically a year's wage for a working man, since the parable of the vineyard indicates that a penny a day was fair pay. Three hundred pence would therefore be wages for fifty weeks of six working days each. John explicitly tells us that it was "very costly." Such ointment would ordinarily be used only for embalming the dead; and then, only by wealthy families. There is ample indication in the Gospel narratives that the family of Lazarus was comfortably off, and almost certainly such a flask of spikenard would have been used in preparing him for the tomb a few days earlier. But Jesus had brought Lazarus forth, and restored him to his family. In gratitude to Him, could Mary give less for His anointing than she had given for embalming the dead body of her brother? On the lowest level of mere human thankfulness, this was a gracious and worthy deed, which should have evoked the abounding pleasure of the disciples; they should have entered into all that it so perfectly expressed, of gratitude and affection, on the part of the re-united and rejoicing family.

"Wherefore this waste," however—the grudging complaint was taken up by the Eleven; for how easily our baser natures respond to suggestions of evil! This cankered criticism came from the bitter spirit and treacherous heart of Judas: and those who should have rebutted it vigorously, re-echoed it. No wonder our Lord had thought it needful to give the warning, "Take heed what ye hear . . ." (Mark 4: 24). But in uttering his cynical words, Judas said more than he realised: for by them he revealed his own condition and pronounced his own doom. It is significant that the word translated "waste" is elsewhere rendered "perdition," and was later applied to Judas by our Lord, in his high-priestly prayer, "the son of perdition" —*son of waste*! He who complained of the "waste" of this moving and beautiful expression of devotion, was himself the supreme example of waste, in all history. He had privileges such as all mankind might envy, as a companion of the Lord, and he wasted them; he had opportunities of highest honour, as an apostle of the Christ and pillar of His Church, and he wasted them; he had supreme prospects in relation to the Kingdom of God, and he wasted them by becoming a traitor. He who might have been a witness of the Resurrection and a messenger of eternal life, went out and hanged himself. His was the waste. We learn from his stark story that by our own words we judge—not others, as we so often think; certainly not the Lord—but ourselves. In our relationship to Jesus, and our reaction to tokens of love and devotion to Him, we reveal our own condition and our true selves.

Our Lord's reply to the whispering was immediate and un-equivocal. "Let her alone," He commanded. Hands off! How dared they by such carnal criticism seek to spoil this splendid token of faith and love? Then the Lord uttered words the full import of which we cannot precisely determine: "against the day of my burying hath she kept this." Had Mary realised that He was about to be crucified, and was she thus signifying her understanding of what He had been so plainly saying? Jesus had explicitly foretold His death, and the manner of it; and that He would rise again on the third day. But the apostles had—like the rest of the nation—so entrenched themselves in their own notions of the Messiah and His Kingdom, that His words could not reach them. They were deaf to His solemn statements, and therefore quite un-prepared for their fulfilment when it came; and now, of course, unable to appreciate the wondrous significance with which Jesus invested Mary's act. Maybe she herself did not anticipate the value which the Lord would attach to her "good work": as Judas spoke more revealingly than he realised, so possibly Mary's act had a depth of significance beyond her intention. That is often the case when we speak of Jesus, or show our love and loyalty to Him. We little know the worth of true devotion, in the eyes of God.

I like to think, however, that Mary, who sat at Jesus' feet, had paid Him the compliment of listening to His words, and believing what He said. And if indeed she realised that He was about to die, then surely she believed also His declaration that He would rise again. She had stood at the grave of her dead brother—dead four days, and stinking: and Jesus, the Resurrection and the Life, had called him forth. It could not be possible that *He* should be holden of death! If in the mystery of the divine will, the Prince and Lord of life should submit to death, then He would triumph over it!

Whether or not the understanding and faith of Mary went thus far, we cannot assuredly say: this we know, that Jesus accepted her anointing as for His burying. She did well in obeying the impulse to make this costly token of her love, for had she missed this opportunity there would be no other. Less than a week later, Jesus died while the day which we now call Good Friday was drawing toward its close, and His body was hurriedly entombed before the Sabbath should begin at 6 p.m. Jewish legalism prohibited the touching of a dead body on the Sabbath; so the women with spices for the embalming had to wait for the morning of the third day—and although they came to the tomb very early, they found it empty, for Jesus had risen! They brought *their* spikenard too late!

We can never be too precipitate, or too lavish, in expressing our love to the Lord Jesus. Too often we quench the impulse, and miss the blessing. Too often we resolve to show our love *tomorrow*, by spending more time in prayer and fellowship with the Lord, and in more diligent study of His Word: but tomorrow is not ours, and the deferred opportunity may never return to us. If we love the Lord, and would manifest our love, *now* is the time to do so. What is spent upon the Lord is never "waste"—though there are ever those ready to suggest that we

77

deprive the needy if we give to the Lord. There is so much to do, they point out, in the Name and service of Christ. We must be busy, and not spend too much time selfishly with our Bibles and upon our knees. But, says the Lord, "the poor always ye have with you." We shall never lack opportunities for service and witness; but more vital, more urgent still is the love we bestow upon *Him*, and the fellowship we enjoy with Him. He longs for our love, our friendship; the fragrance of our true devotion. He invites us to keep Him company in the way. We, too, may pause with Him at Bethany, and proceed with Him along the *Via Dolorosa*. We, too, may heed His word, and walk with Him on the road to the cross. We, too, may share with Mary love's highest privilege, in anointing His head and feet against the day of His burying . . .

13

The King Comes To His City

D ID ever a king have a more extraordinary welcome to his capital city, than Jesus did when He rode into Jerusalem on the foal of an ass, to the shouted greetings of the crowd and the waving of palm branches? We call it now His triumphal entry; but it must have seemed a sorry spectacle to any Roman observer of that unrehearsed rustic parade. Rome had perfected the pomp and military splendour of triumphal processions: the entry of an army commander into Rome after a notable conquest was a spectacle unsurpassed even to our own day. What a contrast to the disciplined, glittering ranks of Rome's legions, attending the magnificent chariots of the victorious general and his suite, was the motley rabble around the benign young provincial on a donkey, shouting and laying their cloaks in His path.

However ludicrous it might have seemed to a Roman, this simple ceremony was more significant to the Jewish people, rulers and rabble alike, than the most elaborate procession. They realised—what no Roman could grasp, unless he had made intensive study of the Jewish religion and Scriptures— that this was indeed a royal entry: and that, in a deliberate fulfilment of the cherished tradition, the Galilean preacher was claiming to be the Messiah, the King of Israel.

Jesus had previously firmly prevented any attempt to acclaim Him as King: now He deliberately arranged this public demonstration in support of His Messianic claims. He sent a disciple with a regal command to the owner of the ass, "The Lord hath need of him," and then rode into the city in such a manner as to evoke the excited greetings, "Hosannah to the Son of David . . . Blessed be the King that cometh in the Name of the Lord . . ." The people saw nothing incompatible between His manner of entering the city and the triumphant greeting they were giving Him. For, humble as the ass may seem to us, it was very differently regarded in Israel. Age-old stories recorded how judges and rulers of honoured memory had travelled through the country by donkey, fulfilling their magisterial duties. The ass therefore had a place of its own in the traditions of the nation and in the esteem of the people. More than that, it was symbolic of a ruler moving among his subjects on missions of peaceful beneficence, rather than in stern judgment: it was essentially associated with peace, as the horse was with war.

There is a reticence in the New Testament narratives which is often very tantalising: questions leap to the lips concerning most of the Gospel stories. So it is here. Who, for instance, was the owner of the ass that Jesus appropriated; and what was his reaction to the demand of the disciples? Some critics of the Bible have suggested that our Lord was high-handed; indeed, that He virtually stole the beast. Unquestionably, however, there is an untold story behind the incident, at which we can only guess. It seems evident that there was some kind of understanding between Jesus and the ass's owner. Maybe he was a disciple, or one who had received benefit from the Lord—perhaps he was one of the many who had been healed by Jesus, and in gratitude had offered hospitality, or help, or even this ass, placing it at the disposal of the Lord should He ever require it.

There can be little doubt, whatever the circumstances, that it was to a man ready to respond that the call came, "The Lord hath need of him." And how proud he would be, to know that his beast carried Jesus in triumph into Jerusalem. True, his pleasure would swiftly give place to perplexity, in the succeeding days of that most notable week in human history: but afterward, how deep would be his gratification that he had shared in some small measure in the events which led up to the cross and the triumphant resurrection of the One who rode in simple majesty the unbroken foal placed at His disposal!

This story behind the Gospel story has an implication and challenge for us: out of gratitude we offer to our Lord all we have and are—and He accepts what we present. But sometimes He says to us, as to this man, "Keep it for me until I am

80

ready to use it." The time will surely come when He will further say, "The Lord hath need . . ." and happy is the servant responding instantly to His behest. For the King of glory delights to use what His servants dedicate to His cause: and therein they are privileged to keep Him company in the way of the cross—and of the triumph He achieved through it.

The drama in miniature enacted around the ass and its owner was a microcosm of the situation presented to the rulers, and to the nation as a whole: Jesus was affirming His claim to be Messiah the King, and the issue was crystal clear—whether to recognise or to refuse His sovereignty. That simple incident, indeed, brings into sharp focus the twofold significance of Palm Sunday: first, the *character* of His sovereignty; and secondly, our *attitude* to Christ the King.

One clear lesson which we learn from a study of the prophetic Scriptures is that the prophetic word is often fully understood only in its fulfilment. Looking back, we can see that all the inspired utterances concerning the coming Messiah, given over a period of hundreds of years, through many lips, were literally fulfilled in Jesus: but we can also see that, before He came, it must have been practically impossible, even for the most spiritually illumined men of God, to reconcile the seemingly contradictory forecasts concerning great David's greater Son, and those of the Lamb of God, stricken and suffering. There were Scriptures which seemed to justify the Jewish expectation of a national deliverer, who would exalt Israel above all the nations; so they fastened all their hopes and expectations on these, and ignored those other Scriptures which presented a different picture.

One such prophecy was Zechariah 9: 9, which Jesus literally fulfilled in riding into Jerusalem on an ass. The prophet declared that the Messiah would be "just (i.e. righteous), and having salvation; lowly, and riding upon an ass, and upon a colt the foal of an ass." So He was; and so He came into the city. "A just God and a Saviour"—Isaiah also had seen the need for such an One (45: 21). In thus claiming to be King, Jesus declared in enacted parable—as well as in fulfilment of the prophetic word—that He had come, not a warlike deliverer from human oppressors, but for peaceful purposes: to release from the oppression of sin, and to establish the reign of righteousness. He had come to *save*: not to fulfil their nationalistic aspirations and worldly ambitions, but to establish among men the Kingdom of God.

That distinction between the true character of His Kingship and their conceptions of Messiah's reign, precipitated the second issue—their attitude toward Him. Extraordinary as it seems to us, the Jewish authorities thought to impose their own terms upon the coming King. In a world where the Roman Emperor exercised despotic sovereignty, so that his least command was obeyed to the ends of the earth, these self-deluded Jews expected a Messiah who would sweep the Romans out of the land, and yet be pliant in their hands. They wanted a king, yet one who would do for them, and give to them, just what they desired: a king, in fact, upon their conditions, not His.

Such a conception of kingship, however, was a contradiction in terms. A king was a sovereign: in those days nothing was known of constitutional monarchy, so they had no excuses for their strange "democratic" notions. Certainly there is no suggestion in the Scriptures of anything other than absolute monarchy, in relation to God and His Christ.

Jesus overthrew all these fantastic Jewish notions of Messiah's reign, and presented Himself as a King requiring allegiance and submission, loyalty and loving obedience. The proud priests were too fond of their own lordly positions and prerogatives, however, to submit themselves to His sovereignty: and because of His claims, and the demands these made upon them, they hated Him and resolved with all their strength of purpose, "We will not have this man to reign over us." Their pride of place and their ambitious prejudices blinded their eyes and animated their hostility toward Him—impelling them along the road to the final rejection, to the awful cry of "Crucify Him," and to the cross. Yes, they too walked that road, harrying and hustling Him to the ignominious tree—and jeering at Him in short-lived triumph as He hung upon it.

They knew full well what His claims were; they knew also the authentication of those claims in the miracles He had wrought: yet with bitter resolution they set themselves against Him, blind and deaf to every reason and every evidence that He was indeed the Christ. Never would they submit to Him as *their* king! They attempted at first to deride His claims, and laugh to scorn the very idea that He was the Messiah; but His Messianic acts and kingly character were acknowledged on every hand; and His kingly demeanour when arraigned before them confounded and embarrassed them to the point of exasperation.

But, however much they wished to set the matter aside as unworthy of serious consideration, they were obliged to state as their formal charge against Him before the Roman Procurator, that He claimed to be king: for on no other ground could they secure a death sentence. And then, to their further embitterment, instead of acceding compliantly to their desires for His death, Pilate presented the challenge of this charge in its most personal aspect: "Shall I crucify your king?"—so that in rage they were obliged to shout, what at other times they would have bitten out their tongues rather than utter: "We have no king but Cæsar!"

Still further increasing the tension of this supreme issue, Pilate made mock of *them* in allowing the soldiery to make mock of Jesus as king of the Jews, robing Him in purple and crowning Him with thorns; and Pilate pierced them to the heart when he exclaimed, with extended finger pointing to the scourged, thorn-crowned prisoner, "Behold your king!" One final act of Roman scorn for their petty jealousies and sinister spite—which was overruled by heaven to set forth for all time and eternity the true significance of what was transpiring, and who it was nailed to the cross—was the placing of the superscription above His head, "This is Jesus of Nazareth, the king of the Jews"—which Pilate refused to alter, despite their strongest pleadings. Thus Israel fulfilled the prophetic word, in joining hands with hated Gentiles in crucifying their Messiah, in slaying the Prince of Life and the Lord of Glory. And in dying, Jesus secured His Kingdom, which shall endure for ever.

This is the message, the abiding significance and challenge of Palm Sunday: Jesus is indeed Christ the King. A day is coming when He shall exercise His sovereignty over all flesh, as King of kings and Lord of lords: to Him every knee shall bow. But we see not yet all things put under Him. In this dispensation of grace, His Kingdom is established in the hearts and lives of those who willingly, gladly crown Him Lord of their lives and God of their salvation. He reigns in grace; He invites into His Kingdom "whosoever will . . ." But His is an absolute monarchy: He exercises His Kingship with the authority of God the Creator-Redeemer.

So many people still, like the Pharisees, desire a Saviour who will do for them just whatever they want; who will forgive their sins and secure for them eternal felicity; One to whom they can turn confidently in time of need, to rescue them from all discomforts—in a word, virtually to be at their command. Instead, He presents Himself as King. To receive Him as Saviour is also to acknowledge Him as Lord. To be born anew by His Spirit is to become a subject of His Kingdom. To come to His cross for pardon, is to kneel at His feet in glad and grateful submission. That is the issue presented by His triumphal entry.

From early days of the Church, the saints have loved to declare that "He reigned from the tree." It was on the cross that He established His sovereignty as the redeemer of men. It is at the cross we make our simplest yet most widely-embracing confession, in the words of a disciple who so strangely delayed to do so: "My Lord and my God."

14

Olivet's Foreglimpse of the Future

HOSTILITY, especially on the part of people we fain would esteem, is hard to bear. The Jews were trained from infancy to regard the priests and scribes with profound respect, for they sat in Moses' seat. Their authority was two-fold: they were—subject to Rome's despised suzerainty—the rulers of the nation, as well as religious leaders. It was a grievous matter to fall foul of the priests. The fact that Jesus of Nazareth had incurred their wrath, and was in open defiance of them, undoubtedly played a large part in the swing of public opinion away from Him, following the initial year of popularity which marked his ministry in Galilee. Ordinary folk, and the more influential, alike feared to be associated with a man at odds with the rulers. The sustained loyalty of the disciples to the Lord, therefore, despite their qualms on this score, is in itself a striking evidence of His command of their deepest convictions and their devoted love, as well as a tribute to their superb courage in continuing as His companions.

The breach between Jesus and the rulers had steadily become wider, until it reached its culmination in His terrible denunciation of them, which must have startled and astounded every listener, and awed even the apostles. Every repetition of the indignant imprecation, "Woe unto you, scribes and Pharisees, hypocrites!" was like the sounding of a knell—only, a knell for *Him*, not for those He was denouncing. The pharisees could not allow such a public denunciation to pass unheeded; and nothing less than His death could assuage their anger.

Then, in one of those swift changes of mood and manner with which His disciples were familiar—even while their ears were still tingling under the impact of the sternest and severest, the most scornful and stinging words ever to be expressed in human speech—He dropped His voice and uttered in broken tones the most tender, yearning, compassionate phrases ever heard among men: "O Jerusalem, Jerusalem, thou that killest the prophets, and stonest them that are sent unto thee, how often would I have gathered thy children together, even as a hen gathereth her chicken under her wings, and ye would not!" It was the heart-cry of the rejected Shepherd. It presaged the pronouncement of their immediate doom: "Behold, your house is left unto you desolate. For I say unto you, Ye shall not see me henceforth till ye shall say, Blessed is He that cometh in the Name of the Lord." And He went out of the temple, never more to enter it.

With their minds and hearts in turmoil, the disciples were eager to ask Him for some clarification of His meaning: but they seemingly did not quite know how to broach the subject. Therefore they began hesitantly "to shew Him the buildings of the temple." He read their thoughts, and replied bluntly, "There shall not be left here one stone upon another, that shall not be thrown down." That was not the place for fuller explanations, however; so He withdrew with them from the precincts of the temple, and from the city, to the quiet slopes of the Mount of Olives, commanding a panoramic view of both city and temple. There they gathered round Him, while He sat and spoke to them of things to come.

The Olivet discourse is, in some respects, the most remarkable of all the teachings of Jesus. Our interest, when we read it, is so focused upon its content, however, that perhaps we tend to overlook the even more remarkable fact that He could deliver it when He did. He knew what the sequel to His condemnation of the rulers would be. He was fully aware that His hour had come, and that ere the week was out He would suffer the most agonising death upon that other hill yonder. This peaceful scene and quiet converse with His friends was but an interlude between His spiritually exhausting combat with the authorities and their swift revenge. Moreover, He had not uttered His condemnation of them without cost to Himself. Let us ever remember that the Lord Jesus was not a steely moralist, who half-enjoyed—as some do—the denunciation of the guilty. He was the Messiah of Israel, despised and rejected of men, yet sorrowing over their sin with the love of the lost which had brought Him from heaven and would take Him to Calvary. But with steady gaze He looked beyond that "green hill without the city wall" to the triumph and the glory which should follow. Never was Jesus more sublime in His faith as Son of Man, and more inspiring to His followers as Son of God, than in that hour on Olivet.

In extent, the Olivet discourse ranks third among His recorded addresses. Only the Sermon on the Mount, with which He began His public instruction of the disciples, and the sequence of conversational discourses with which He closed His private preparation of them for the ordeal of the cross— recorded in John's Gospel alone—exceed in length the discourse recorded in Matthew 24 and 25. It is, of course, essentially apocalyptic; and concerning its interpretation there are widely differing views. With those controversial aspects we are not now concerned: our purpose is to consider briefly what was clear and plain in our Lord's message to the anxious group of men around Him; and what is of perennial significance for His Church in all the generations since.

The most striking characteristic of this survey of events, reaching to the very end of the age, is the calm assumption of omniscience by Jesus. He speaks with absolute and unequivocal authority upon the entire course of human history, and its culmination in the realised eternal purposes of God—and all in relation to Himself as the guide and goal of all. This is manifestly either the word of incarnate God, or the fantastical illusion of the most audacious imposter the world has ever seen. Second only to this note of finality, is the equally firm assertion that all human affairs are under the sovereign and guiding hand of God; that He is directing all events of history to His chosen and appointed ends; and that He is working His purposes out despite the confusion and chaos of man's making, and even of the seeming triumphs of evil. Timely and comforting as was that confidence to the harassed and fearful apostles, it is no less relevant and reassuring to us today.

The discourse began with the answers of Jesus to a twofold question, "When shall these things—His forecast of the destruction of the temple—be; and what shall be the sign of Thy coming and of the end of the world?" Now, we recognise readily enough the distinction between the two parts of this question; and, indeed, that our Lord treated—and answered—them as if they were two separate and distinct questions. To the disciples, however, these were almost certainly two ways of asking one question: they thought that the destruction of the city and His return would coincide, and would mark "the end of the age." In their eagerness, their questionings spilled out of them: they endeavoured to convey their half-formed thought first in one way and then in another; but it was one event they thought He had foretold, and about which they wished to know more.

Very often in the Lord's words there is more than we apprehend. So it was with the Twelve. He answered their questions in all the range of their implications—even although the inquirers had no conception of those wider aspects. They understood enough in His reply, however, for the realisation of His immediate purposes, and for their comfort and instruction; and the Church through all subsequent centuries has found inspiration and guidance in the words which Jesus intended for future readers rather than those first hearers of them.

Now, in discussing the destruction of the temple and of the city, and also the then far-future end of the age, our Lord did not point out that these events would be separated by long centuries: that would have confused and troubled the disciples. Indeed, nowhere in Scripture is there explicit intimation of this two-millennial Church age, although we can—wise after the event—discern many indications of it in the teaching of our Lord, and also in the subsequent revelation given through the apostles.

As Jesus spoke, therefore—and unquestionably as they continued to do afterward—the Twelve took for granted that the entire discourse related to events which they assumed would happen very soon. It is no part of our present purpose to try to differentiate between those sections of the discourse which relate to AD 70 and those which will find fulfilment only at the Second Advent of our Lord. Admittedly, the two seem sometimes to inter-twine, and students are not agreed in their unravelling. What is of supreme significance is this: that when Titus was about to invest the city, the Church understood aright the Lord's message to them concerning it, and—they alone of all the inhabitants of Jerusalem—fled the city, and so escaped the horrors of that time of tribulation. Likewise, I am convinced, the true Church at the end of the age will recognise the signs He gave of His impending appearing, when He is "at the doors."

Of special relevance for us is the series of admonitions He gave, concerning our attitude and conduct as His disciples in the period between these two climactic events. In a series of graphic metaphors and arresting parables, He stressed the necessity of watchfulness for His appearing and faithfulness in His service. As the servants of a Lord who is making a journey in a far country, we have a charge to keep and a duty to fulfil: and blessed is that servant who, when his Lord cometh, shall be found so doing.

The coming of the Lord is certain as the dawn. The Blessed Hope of the Church is based upon His sure word, and is essential to the achievement of His ultimate purposes. Jesus on Olivet was answering the most vital questionings not only of the Twelve, but of His people through all ages—and setting before them the glorious prospect of His return in triumph unthwarted of all ill. Jesus of Nazareth, rejected of Israel as their Messiah, is nevertheless great David's greater Son; King of kings and Lord of lords. He must reign: to that end He will come again, in power and great glory, to establish His Kingdom in all the earth. Despite apostasy and schism and heresy within, and persecution without, His Church shall endure to the end, and will greet Him with joy unspeakable at His appearing—a great multitude which no man can number, out of every tribe and nation, without spot or wrinkle or any such thing: His Body and His Bride. His people are on the winning side!

But what, some might ask, has this to do with the road to the cross? Far more than the fact that Jesus gave this survey of future events within a few hours of His condemnation to the cross: *it was upon that cross, and what He accomplished there, that this course of future events totally depended.* It was only in virtue of His substitutionary death upon the cross, that such further purposes of grace for fallen mankind could be envisaged and effected. The cross is not only the pivot of history, but also of the realisation of the divine purposes for the eternal destiny of mankind. All that our Lord foretold presupposed the cross. On Olivet He had Golgotha in full view. But the cross had never been for Him an end, but only a means to an end. He was not only treading the road to the cross, but the road which led to the open tomb and an opened door into heaven. He was not only ready to endure the cross, but was able to look, by faith, beyond it—far beyond it, right unto that day when He shall see of the travail of His soul and be gloriously, eternally satisfied. The radiance of Golgotha illumines Olivet, and imparts to its message not only its deep note of challenge but also its ring of triumph.

15

A Meal with the Twelve

NOTHING is more striking in the entire story of the life of Jesus, than His spirit of calm detachment and self forgetfulness under the very shadow of the cross. That He was not regardless of, or somehow superior to, the human travail of His impending Passion, we shall see as we accompany Him to the Garden: but in the upper room, an hour or two before, we find Him manifesting supremely "a heart at leisure from itself," and utterly devoted to the concerns of His Kingdom, and of His disciples. Yet He was aware, not only of the determination of the rulers to kill Him, but of the treachery of Judas in having covenanted with His enemies to betray Him. Because of that foul plot, indeed, the Lord had to make arrangements in secret for the Passover meal with His disciples, to prevent Judas from doing his treacherous work beforehand, and so to ensure that the upper room should not be violated by the breaking-in of a mob to arrest Him. At the last minute, therefore, He sent two of the disciples to meet a man who, by pre-arrangement, would be carrying a water-pot, and would act as their guide to the house—presumably belonging to a resident in Jerusalem who was among His unnamed disciples—where a guest-chamber had been placed at His disposal. There they were to make ready—and whether or not it was the actual Passover meal they prepared, the Evangelists make plain that our Lord so regarded it.

When He arrived at the upper room with the rest of the disciples, Jesus at once brought home to them the particular character of this last meal they would have together, before His cross, by saying, "With desire I have desired to eat this Passover with you before I suffer." There is a twofold note in this deeply moving expression of His yearning for their human companionship and spiritual fellowship. First, there was surely an intensely personal note, of longing for this brief respite from the tension of the week and the travail that was so swiftly to follow, in the loving and loyal comradeship of the Eleven around the meal table. Judas would be there for a time, it is true, to mar the peace and the brotherliness of it: but after his withdrawal there would be an hour of most precious communion with the true-hearted men who, for all their faults, were nevertheless His devoted friends and followers. There was also a note of Messianic purpose in our Lord's words: for He never allowed personal considerations to deflect Him in the least from the fulfilling of the Father's will. He knew what this meal in the upper room would mean in future days, not only to the Eleven, but to the Church through all the centuries. He foreknew what instruction He would give, what imperishable words He would utter, what a lesson in action He would impart; also the sacrament of the new covenant which He would initiate. All this He did, in surpassing disregard of the distress which—as also He knew—the next few hours would hold for Him. St. John gives us the secret of His sublime self-negation: "Having loved His own . . ." the apostle tells us, "He loved them unto the end," i.e., *unto the utmost degree* (13: 1).

A jarring note was sounded right at the beginning, however. The disciples, who despite their close bonds of common discipleship to the Lord, nevertheless often squabbled about their future places in the Kingdom, now disputed about "which of them should be accounted the greatest." There is some little doubt as to precisely when, during the evening, this "strife" occurred; but almost certainly it arose concerning their order of precedence at the table, as they were taking their places. How much fellowship is marred, and witness spoiled, by self-aggrandisement and self-seeking; by squabbles about punctilios and priorities! On this occasion, their dispute evoked the most notable lesson ever given on the Christian grace of humility. For, laying aside His garments, Jesus took a basin of water and began to wash the disciples' feet. As preface to the story, however, John observes that "the devil having now put it into the heart of Judas . . . to betray Him; Jesus, knowing that the Father had given all things into His hands, and that He was come from God and went to God, He riseth from supper . . . and took a towel, and girded Himself . . ." It was in the full consciousness that His hour had come; that Judas was about to betray Him; that all authority and might were His by right of His eternal Godhead; that He was the only-begotten Son incarnate, and would soon resume His place in the midst of the throne on high—in the realisation of all this, Jesus, in the voluntary humiliation of His humanity, stooped to the posture and fulfilled the duty of a household slave. Not one of that company had been ready to perform this office for the rest. All had waited for someone else to take the lowly place and render the menial service of washing their feet; and as no one was prepared to assume the rôle of servant to his fellows, the Lord Himself—the Lord of glory—knelt to wash their feet.

In embarrassed silence they watched as He passed from one to another: without doubt each of them felt almost overwhelmed with confusion and shame as their Master took, first one foot and then the other, washing and gently wiping them. All would have welcomed some movement, some gesture, some initiative on the part of another, to take the basin and towel from His hands, and proceed with the task: but none was prepared to be the one to do it. And so Jesus drew near to Peter. That forthright man's consternation was mounting. How could the others possibly endure it! How could they allow Jesus, their Master, to wash their feet! It was all wrong: it should be the other way round; they—any one of them—should be washing *His* feet! But now Jesus was kneeling before him. "Lord," whispered the disconcerted Peter, scarcely knowing how to express his sense of the incongruity of the situation, "does *Thou* wash my feet?" Jesus answered, so quietly and kindly, speaking to the turmoil of the apostle's mind and heart, and indicating that there was something far more important in this act than a rebuke of their churlishness and a lesson in humility and brotherly service: "What I do thou knowest not now; but thou shalt know hereafter." Peter quickly recovered something of his customary aplomb, and blurted out with characteristic impetuosity: "Thou shalt never wash my feet!" Again the Lord quietly indicated that this act of His had a symbolic significance as well as a practical lesson to impart: "If I wash thee not, thou hast no part with me." His mind in a whirl, unable to grasp the real meaning of the Lord's words, Peter swung from one extreme to the other, in his impulsive fashion, and exclaimed, "Lord, not my feet only, but also my hands and my head." Peter was no profound thinker: he felt himself quite out of his depth; but the mere suggestion of the possibility of having "no part" with the Lord called forth his horrified response. There was never any shadow of doubt regarding *his* love and loyalty. With patient gentleness, therefore, Jesus explained, "He that is bathed needeth not save to wash his feet, but is clean every whit: and ye are clean, but not all"—and John adds, "For He knew who should betray Him: therefore said He, Ye are not all clean."

Then, having completed His task, Jesus addressed them all. "Know ye what I have done to you?" He asked; and proceeded, "Ye call me Master and Lord: and ye say well; for so I am. If I then, your Lord and Master, have washed your feet, ye also ought to wash one another's feet. For I have given you an example, that ye should do as I have done to you." Therein He bequeathed to them, and to all who follow in their train, a lesson in humility of mind and graciousness in service, which should be as a guiding star to our conduct through all our days. But our Lord had not completed His enforcement of the lesson: "Verily, verily, I say unto you, the servant is not greater than his lord . . . If ye know these things, happy are ye if ye do them." And remember, Judas was among those whose feet He washed.

It was in a chastened mood that they proceeded with supper, probably chatting restrainedly among themselves, until Jesus suddenly declared, "Verily I say unto you, that one of you shall betray me!" They were dumbfounded, and "exceeding sorrowful." Not that the Eleven thought for a moment that any one of them would play the traitor in such a manner as Judas had, in fact, already pledged himself to do: they probably thought that the Lord meant simply that one of them would, through some foolish or impetuous act "let Him down" and become the means of delivering Him into the hands of His enemies. They knew themselves well enough to ask—every one of them—"Lord, is it I?" To cover up his treachery, Judas joined in and asked the question with the rest. Looking him straight in the eye, Jesus replied, "Thou hast said." The other disciples evidently did not observe this exchange, for still the subdued questioning proceeded; and Peter asked John—who was next to Jesus, and actually leaning his head on the Lord's breast—of whom it was that He spoke. So John looked up into the face of Jesus and whispered, "Lord, who is it?" And Jesus replied, "He it is, to whom I shall give a sop, when I have dipped it." No one else heard, however, for even after the departure of Judas they thought he had just gone out shopping.

The giving of the sop was not merely an indication to John, however; it was a final gesture of appeal to Judas to abandon his evil course and renew his loyalty even at this late hour: for the giving of a sop to a guest by the host, was the supreme expression of friendship at a feast. It was love's last endeavour to win a soul self-abandoned to Satan. Through these past weeks and months of increasing estrangement on the part of Judas, the Lord had never once exposed to the Eleven his change of heart, and his dishonest dealings. With the gradual fading of his ambitious hopes of greatness in the Messianic kingdom he had expected Jesus to establish, Judas had become resentful and antagonistic, and by way of compensation had sought to enrich himself by stealing from their common funds. Yet the Lord did not denounce him, by word or deed. Right to the eleventh hour—and beyond it—He sought to redeem and win this man, despite all the evil he had embraced and the light he had spurned. Thus He loved even Judas unto the end—to the ultimate degree. His final effort spurned, however, He commanded sternly, "That thou doest, do quickly." There is a "sin unto death" which spells eternal doom: the irrevocable decision is made, and the ultimate offer of grace rejected. So Judas went out, into the blackest night of all history.

Judas withdrawn, an inexpressible peace came upon the little group, still assembled round the table, encompassing them in a sweetness of fellowship surpassing anything they had ever before known. In the solemn hush of that unprecedented hour, Jesus took bread, and broke it, and gave it to them, speaking the ever-memorable words, fraught with unfathomable significance: "This is my body, which is given for you: this do in remembrance of me." Then He took the cup, bidding them all to drink of it—again with the thrice-precious words of institution: "This cup is the new covenant in my blood, which is shed for many for the remission of sins"—and adding once more the haunting phrase, "This do ye, as often as ye drink it, in remembrance of me." And implicit in those words was the glorious affirmation of the apostle, which links "that dark betrayal night" with the last advent "in one blest chain of loving rite"—"For as often as ye eat this bread, and drink this cup, ye do shew the Lord's death, till He come."

Then Jesus added the somewhat cryptic remark, "But I say unto you, I will not drink henceforth of this fruit of the vine, until that day when I drink it new with you in my Father's Kingdom." He was unquestionably anticipating that great day when He shall "see of the travail of His soul, and be satisfied" in the completion of the Church and His union with the Bride, at the "marriage of the Lamb." And lest we interpret the language of symbolism too literally, it is significant that almost immediately afterwards He spoke to the Eleven— on the way to the Garden—of Himself as the true vine, and the much fruit He would have them to bear, as branches in that vine. Surely it is *that* "fruit of the vine" He meant. He was anticipating the joy of realisation of all the purposes of God in His redeemed people, through His humiliation and travail. Moreover, He saw in that glad day the full attainment of all that was anticipated and foreshadowed in the Passover. That feast was not merely commemorative of the deliverance from Egypt, but prophetic of the far greater deliverance, into a far better land of promise, through the blood of the Lamb of God. The true Passover Lamb suffered not in vain! Through old covenant and new He proceeded to His appointed goal.

Then, in most intimate, almost awesome, tenderness of fellowship, Jesus gave to the Eleven the imperishable counsel and comfort, commandment and warning, recorded by John alone, in his chapters 13 and 14. The Master had them thus gathered around Him for instruction as His disciples for the last time; preparing them for the testings through which they were so soon to pass, and equipping them for the glorious service they were afterward to render. He hid nothing of the ordeal they were to endure; but He gave assurance of triumph and empowering and highest privilege, beyond the valley of the shadow. The transformation thus of the querulous, aggressive group of so short a time before, was indeed a triumph of His "love to the utmost degree."

96

They must have been reluctant to end that strangely subdued yet ineffably wondrous hour of fellowship at His feet.
But His hour had come: the hour of which He had so often
spoken, and to which all His thoughts and words and ways
had been directed from the beginning. But before He said,
"Arise, let us be going," they sang a hymn. Singing, in such
an hour? under such a shadow—of a cross? Yes, a hymn:
almost certainly Psalms 116–118, the latter part of the *Hallel*,
customarily sung at the Passover. In these psalms David, the
shepherd and sweet singer of Israel, expressed the rejoicing
of the people in the wondrous grace of God their Saviour. As
the little group went out, the upper room was still re-echoing
to the words, "O give thanks unto the Lord, for He is good:
for His mercy endureth for ever."

16

Prayer in a Garden

FROM the supper-room, Jesus went with the Eleven to keep His rendezvous with Judas in the Garden. He knew what would happen there; and Judas knew that He knew. It may seem strange that Judas did not doubt that He would proceed thither: surely anyone with any inkling that such treacherous work was afoot, would avoid the place where it could be perpetrated—and Jesus had given Judas more than an inkling of His comprehension. Yet He went to Gethsemane; and Judas apparently had no fear in his mind that Jesus might not be there—or he would not have risked leading the mob sent by the chief priests to arrest Him, for their anger would have blazed out against himself had the garden been empty. Perhaps Judas had sensed the Lord's set purpose in having "steadfastly set His face toward Jerusalem." He had spoken plainly enough about being arrested and killed; that very fact, indeed, had incensed Judas, who expected the Lord to adopt a regal, rather than—as he would think—a defeatist attitude. However that may be, to Gethsemane Jesus went. Before Judas should arrive, with his traitorous kiss, however, Jesus had one final, supreme act of filial submission to make, in receiving from the hand of His Father the "cup" of His Passion; one final act of devotion and obedience as man, in which His human shrinking from the cross would be subordinated, albeit at the cost of sweat as great drops of blood, to the sublime self-dedication, "Not my will, but Thine, be done."

With the Eleven, then, Jesus left the supper-room, after singing the psalms of the Great Hallel; and, passing through the city, tarried awhile near the temple, where He spoke so wondrously of Himself as the true vine, and of them—His disciples—as the branches, and His Father as the Husbandman who prunes with tender concern, that they might become increasingly fruitful. Perhaps it was there also that He uttered His high-priestly prayer, committing them into the hands of the Father, in the ordeal through which they were to pass; and not only them, but praying also for all who should believe in Him through their word—right on to the end of time. Then, crossing the Kidron, they came to the Mount of Olives and the Garden of Gethsemane, where the Lord had frequently found respite from the tension and turmoil of this past terrible week, and the spiritual refreshment of fellowship with His Father.

In the Garden we are on holy ground. As we contemplate our Saviour's agony, reverent reticence would silence all comment: our most seemly response is to kneel in obedience to His behest, "Watch and pray . . ." The events of the Garden are recorded for our learning, however; we honour the Lord more by heeding the lessons of the story, than we would by well-meaning neglect.

The intense longing of Jesus for the companionship of the apostles is singularly impressive, at a time when, alas, from the very nature of the events which were transpiring, they were least able to give it. This wistful note of yearning had been strongly sounded earlier in the evening: "With desire I have desired to eat this Passover with you before I suffer . . .": here it reaches its highest pitch—"My soul is exceeding sorrowful, even unto death: tarry ye here, and watch with me" (Matt. 26: 38). He needs must face *alone* the issue before Him: even from the three who ever came closest to Him in understanding and intimacy, Jesus withdrew about a stone's throw (Luke 22: 41), to grapple with the issue of all that was immediately entailed for Him personally in embracing the cross. Yet, while He must endure the ordeal alone, He longed to realise the near presence, the human compassion and spiritual fellowship—yes, the support in prayer—of these men who were His friends and companions. Human compassion and sympathetic understanding can be factors of inestimable value in spiritual crises; and though every soul must face ultimate issues alone, Christian fellowship has an incalculable contribution to make, even in such hours.

Alas, how few are able to give it! For something more is required than friendliness and goodwill. In all spiritual crises there are spiritual forces and factors, of which we have little understanding; and merely human qualities will not avail. The apostles were well-intentioned, but despite the Lord's earnest request, they fell asleep. There is a deeply poignant note in the Lord's reproachful question, "Could ye not watch with me one hour?" This was addressed, apparently, to all three; but Matthew records that it was explicitly said to Peter (v. 40), who had just declared so vehemently the superiority of his loyalty over that of all other disciples (Mark 14: 29). According to our privilege, and our profession, will commensurate response be required of us. However, instead of rebuking the sleepy disciples, the Lord found an excuse for them which they were too shamefaced to utter for themselves: "The spirit indeed is willing, but the flesh is weak." Unaided, the flesh can never endure the stress of spiritual travail: to keep "awake" in such situations, we needs must "watch and pray, lest we enter into temptation." How often must the Lord, who thus excused the weary disciples, make excuses for those who should have learned from them the lesson of watchfulness in the hour of evil! But despite this tender word, theirs was the loss; they failed in the supreme opportunity of their discipleship, to succour and sustain the Lord Jesus when He most needed their help. The Lord of glory needs the friendship and spiritual service of sinful men: that is the measure of His grace, and of our privilege—and of our failure, if we sleep when we should watch and pray.

Equally arresting as His desire for their fellowship, is the change in the demeanour of the Lord in the Garden, from that which had characterised His whole life and ministry, and particularly its final phase as He journeyed to Jerusalem, knowing that a cross awaited Him there. He had pursued His way with calm serenity, save on one occasion at the beginning of that last journey from Galilee, when He went before the Twelve in manifest stress of spirit, and "they were amazed; and as they followed, they were afraid. And He . . . began to tell them what things should happen unto Him . . ." (Mark 10: 32). Apart from that solitary indication of strong emotion, as He submitted His will to that of the Father, even in the way of the cross, Jesus pursued that road with majestic calm and steadfast purpose, speaking of the cross to His disciples in such

a way that, though they were sorrowful, they were not alarme
—and the least sign of fear in Him would have caused panic
among them. Thus He had come to Bethany; thus He entered
Jerusalem as Messiah the King; thus He sustained His ministry
of instruction and appeal amid all the hostility and tension of
that last week; thus in sublime self-forgetfulness He kept the
Passover and instituted the sacrament of the new covenant;
thus He made His way to the Garden—right to its very gate,
still comforting and instructing the Eleven: so truly human, so
graciously divine! Then, in the Garden, we see almost a
different person: distressed, even in agony, sweating as it were
great drops of blood. How can we explain this startling
change?

Our Lord's words concerning the way of the cross in relation
to His disciples, supplies the key to His own poise and serenity
when walking therein. "If any man will come after me," He
had said, "*let him deny himself,* and take up his cross, and follow
me" (Matt. 16: 24). Now, we tend to degrade the term, "to
deny oneself," and make it mean simply the forgoing of something we like—denying ourselves sugar in tea, for instance.
As used by Jesus, however, it means *to disregard one's own
interests,* or *to say "no" to oneself.* In effect, to leave oneself out
of account. That is just what Jesus did. His self-committal
to the will of His Father was so absolute, that He fulfilled that
will in total disregard of personal considerations. That is the
spirit of the cross. One of the disturbing features of Evangelical
life in Britain today is the fact that some who have most to say
about the cross, are also most self-centred. The true significance
of our identification with Christ in His cross, however, was
expressed by Dr. D. M. M'Intyre, son-in-law of Dr. Andrew
Bonar, when he said that the cross in our experience means,
"not the abasement of self for self's sake, but the forgetting of
self for love's sake." The *forgetting of self*: that is the secret of
our Saviour's serenity when walking the road to the cross.

When He came to the Garden, however, this self-abnegation
was temporarily set aside, for He must now receive the dread
"cup" by a deliberate act of His own will. We also, no matter
how true our acceptance of the cross might be, nevertheless
must face issues in all the weakness and recoil of our human
personalities. And the glimpse we have of the travail of Jesus,

in bringing His heart and mind to perfect willingness for the cross and all it entailed, is to us, paradoxically, one of the most profoundly comforting and reassuring passages in all Scripture, in times of testing. For by it we know that our Lord was not carried along His appointed way by a lofty superiority to our human weakness and struggles. By it we know that we have not an High Priest who cannot be touched with the feeling of our infirmities, but one who was in all points tempted like as we are—tempted in the Garden, as well as in the wilderness; from the frailty of our human frame, as well as from the malice of the devil. The Captain of our salvation was made perfect through sufferings; and in that He Himself hath suffered being tempted, He is able to succour them that are tempted (Heb. 2: 10, 18).

Mr. Geoffrey T. Bull, the young Brethren missionary who spent three years in Chinese Communist prisons, telling of his ordeal, confessed that the prolonged "brain-washing" brought him practically to breaking-point; and he acknowledged that, when faith had almost gone, "it was not my hold of Him, but His hold of me," which carried him through. Jesus faced ultimate issues; He was in an agony, and sweated great drops of blood: and now, as our High Priest, He knows our frame and frailties, and all the testings we are called upon to endure; and He is able to succour every child of His, even in the severest ordeals of human experience. Blessed be God, Jesus suffered, being tempted . . . and is able to save unto the uttermost. That is the abiding significance for us of the agony of the Garden.

Perhaps the most moving event in all the story of the Passion is the recoil of Jesus, in His true humanity, from the horror and shame of the cross. The anticipation was even more terrible than the actual enduring of it—as is so often the case with experiences through which His people pass. He naturally shrank from its pain and manifold distresses; but it was doubtless the dereliction of the sin-bearer which evoked His agonised prayer, "Father, if it be possible, let this cup pass from me." How often we echo such a cry, in our infinitely lesser ordeals: "O God, Thou art Almighty, and canst deliver me. . . ." But God cannot violate His own will and purpose, for His Son or for us; and so Jesus proceeded at once to submit His will, shrinking as He did from the bitter cross, to that purpose of the Father—"nevertheless not my will, but Thine, be done." In that response of faith and submission, He exemplified for us the way of filial obedience and of victory. But we do not read that His soul was instantly filled with peace and restored poise: rather we see Him kneel in prayer a second time, repeating the same words; then yet again, the third time. And here we have one of the most vital lessons of all Scripture concerning prayer. Our Lord had earlier declared the worthlessness of vain repitition; but He had also stressed the necessity for importunity in prayer. Even when the right words are uttered, in the right spirit, the battle is not necessarily ended and the victory won. The peace which passes all understanding does not always immediately attend the word of submission. There is need for persistence in prayer; for tarrying in the presence of God; for repeating our affirmation of faith, until our will is truly—without any reservation—one with His will: then the peace of God fills the soul, and serenity pervades the entire personality.

So it was with Jesus. After He had prayed the third time, the turmoil was ended, and He went onward to His cross in such majestic calm as had previously sustained Him. His was the ascendant spirit when the rabble arrived, and were awe-struck by His truly regal demeanour. He was the dominating figure in the travesties of trials before religious leaders, puppet king, and Roman procurator. Enraged by His fearless calm and manifest superiority of spirit, which exposed their baseness, these representatives of human justice disgraced their offices in subjecting Him to the most degrading indignities; and through them all He manifested the inward calm and outward dignity which flowed from His utter dedication to the will of God. If we would know something of such a spirit, we must seek it through oft-repeated prayer, as did our Lord.

It was in such poise of spirit that He received the traitor's kiss. How it must have burned His cheek! But He suffered it— as He has suffered many a one since. For treachery is ever ready to kiss when it is about to betray; and it is only an intimate acquaintance who can do so dastardly a deed. Alas, the Church has had many a Judas in its ranks, and has so still. Let all who harbour resentment and bitterness remember in time the terrible lengths to which they are capable of driving even avowed disciples of the Lord.

If Judas betrayed, Peter at least showed courageous loyalty by slashing out wildly with his sword, cutting off the ear of one of those laying hold of Jesus to arrest Him. But the Lord, in full command of the perilous situation, told His impetuous disciple to put up his sword: for His Kingdom was not of this world, else would His servants fight. Then, in an act of supernal grace, in utter self-denying, He reached out His hand and touched the ear of Malchus, performing His last miracle of physical healing, as He uttered the words, "Suffer ye thus far . . ."—"allow me enough freedom from my bonds to do this." Amazing grace, to heal one who had come to lead Him to trial and mockery and the cross. Amazing grace He ever manifests toward sinners, equally undeserving: it determined the struggle with His own shrinking from the cross in the Garden; and it reaches out to every guilty heart in all the world, which will respond to it and receive it.

17

Jewish and Gentile Judges

HUMAN nature is revealed in its true character in the presence of Jesus Christ. He calls forth the best in every life that He touches; and He exposes the worst. In most lives there are potentialities for good and for evil which are seldom fully revealed. But God sees what is hidden from our fellow men. The Word of God insists, in Old Testament and New, that He looks on the heart, and knows the innermost thoughts. He knows the unexpressed longings and aspirations, the desire for good which all too often we fail to achieve; and the ineffable comfort comes to us from His throne of grace, that He accepts our true intent, even if it is not fully effected. And Jesus of Nazareth, God incarnate, read the thoughts and knew what was in the hearts of men—both good and bad. More than that, He called forth even in the most shy and reticent what they otherwise would hesitate to express: think of the faith of the woman with the issue of blood; the repentance of the woman who was a sinner; and the restitution made by Zacchaeus. Not only did our Lord evoke hitherto suppressed potentialities for good, however, but He brought into the open the hidden evil of hearts. Scribes and Pharisees might disguise their avaricious activities and selfish schemings behind a façade of hypocrisy and feigned zeal for the Law; but Jesus stripped off the mask and exposed them for what they were. That is why they hated Him, and sought His death. His exposure of their true characters became more outspoken and more devastating as His ministry proceeded, until it reached its final scathing, scarifying denunciation in His repeated pronouncement of woe upon them. Determined to silence this alarming voice, they brought Him to trial—and therein, confronted with Jesus, they were fully revealed, as in a mirror, for the men they were.

First, He was taken to Annas, the crafty, scheming Sadducee who had been turned out of the high-priestly office by the Romans, because of his intrigues. He was the father-in-law of Caiaphas, the present high-priest, but still the "grey eminence," the power behind the high-priestly throne. Apparently he occupied a wing or part of the high-priestly palace. The appearance of Christ before him was informal, however, and nothing is told us about it. Perhaps, like Herod, Annas desired to see the One of whom he had heard so much, whom he half-feared, and over whom he wanted to exercise his sense of power. While this unofficial arraignment of Jesus before Annas was taking place, the members of the Sanhedrin were being hurriedly assembled despite the untimely hour, in the court-room of the official residence. Thither Jesus was taken. This gathering was quite illegal, such a sitting of the court during the night being expressly forbidden by the Law. These men, however, whose rigid enforcement of meaningless legal trivialities had been so sternly denounced by Jesus, were ready for any violation of the fundamental precepts of the Law in order to achieve their evil ends.

The proceedings began with an interrogation of Jesus by Caiaphas, concerning His disciples and teaching—implying that He had been fostering a secret and subversive movement. Our Lord rebutted this insidious suggestion vigorously and bluntly: "I spake openly to the world; I ever taught in the synagogue and in the temple, whither the Jews always resort; and in secret I have said nothing. Why askest thou me? Ask them which heard me, what I have said unto them: behold, they know what I have said" (John 18: 20, 21). The assembly was startled: these august dignitaries were accustomed to deferential pleadings, not to such stinging satire. One of the outraged officials struck our Lord, exclaiming, "Answerest Thou the high priest so?" Strange conduct that, for a law court; but it passed unrebuked by the priestly judges. Then these wicked men, who had schemed to pervert the justice they were entrusted to exercise, by arranging for false witnesses to testify against Jesus, had the exasperating experience of hearing their bribed witnesses contradict one another, and so cancel out the effect of their perjured testimony. The entire proceedings were about to collapse, when Caiaphas broke in with mock indignation, pretending to be distressed by the weight of "evidence" against the Prisoner, and saying, "Answerest Thou nothing? What is this that they testify against Thee?" But Jesus saw through his device, and remained silent. Frustrated, and frightened of losing his prey even when in his very hands, Caiaphas played his last card. Solemnly and formally putting the Prisoner upon oath, according to the Jewish Law, he said, "I adjure Thee by the living God, that Thou tell us whether Thou be the Christ, the Son of God." Here was the heart of the matter and the crux of the trial. Standing before the religious leaders and supreme rulers and authorities of Israel, Jesus bore unequivocal testimony: "I am." Lest there should be any misunderstanding of the character and range of His claims, He added, "Hereafter shall ye see the Son of Man sitting on the right hand of power, and coming in the clouds of heaven" (Mark 14: 55–62). He, arraigned before them, declared Himself to be the eternal Lord and Judge of all. Thus before the highest court of Israel, Jesus bore witness that He was the Messiah, the Son of God Most High. In that moment the destiny of the nation hung in the balance. He had preached to multitudes in all parts of the land; but this group of men held the reins of power, religiously: it was their responsibility to decide whether Israel should formally acknowledge or reject Him as the Christ. He had come unto His own; but they received Him not. Despite all the testimony of His life, His words, and His deeds, they would not have Him as *their* Lord. In the violence of their rejection of His Person and His claims they lost all self-control, screaming at Him, striking Him, and spitting in His face (v. 65). In that terrible display of basest passions, the religious leaders of the Jews were revealed in their true character. Their conduct is the most solemn lesson in all history concerning the blindness, self-deception, arrogance, and even enmity against God, which may flourish in the name of religion, and even be engendered by it. It is the most stark demonstration of the fact that to be religious is not necessarily to be godly, or even merely good. Religion, in fact, was Christ's first, most persistent, most bitter adversary; it may ever be the greatest snare to His people, as it has unquestionably been to His Church throughout the centuries, despite the warnings and admonitions of the Gospel story.

Thus were the religious leaders of Israel made manifest in the presence of Jesus: their every sham and disguise, and all their veneer, was stripped off, and they declared themselves in deeds and words precisely for what they were—selfish, shameless, ungodly, even devilish. By their judgment upon Jesus they judged themselves, at the bar of history, and of heaven's high throne.

Desirous as they were of bringing about the death of Jesus, the Sanhedrin could not carry out their intent, for the Romans had taken away from them the power to inflict the capital penalty. They had therefore to transfer the case to the court of the procurator. It would seem that they had been in communication with Pontius Pilate, and expected him—as a mere formality—to confirm the sentence which they had, in effect, passed upon Him. Their evident confusion when Pilate made clear his intention of conducting a full trial according to Roman law, indicates how unready they were for this. "If He were not a malefactor," they blustered, "we would not have delivered Him up to thee." That would not do for Pilate, however; so he said, "Take ye Him, and judge Him according to your law." Then they showed their hand: "It is not lawful for us to put any man to death," they replied—and Pilate saw in a moment that nothing less would satisfy them. He had no compunction toward any Jew, and no hesitation in ordering the crucifixion of any; but somehow he was reluctant to "do their dirty work for them"—the crude colloquial phrase probably expresses precisely how he felt. By now, however, the Jewish authorities had gathered their wits, and preferred the charge against Jesus, that He had fomented insurrection, claiming to be a king. There could be no more serious indictment, in the Roman Empire of those days; with only the flimsiest support, it could ensure the death penalty. Pilate, however, had seen through them: he knew well that they had no zeal for the Roman authority, but that "for envy they had delivered Him" (Mark 15: 10). Ever at loggerheads with these arrogant ecclesiastics, Pilate was loath to yield to their will; but also, he was reluctant to offend them, knowing how ready they would be to complain of him to Rome, and that might make trouble. And so the "trial" was degraded to a verbal tussle, a tug-of-war of wills between Pilate and the Jewish leaders: the issue involved, the true exercise of justice, was subordinated to the struggle for power between these antagonistic personalities. One vital matter became crystal-clear, however: the charge made against the prisoner was that He claimed to be a king, and on that Pilate fastened, in all his questioning of Jesus, all his comments concerning Him, and finally, in his writing of the superscription for the cross. And just as Jesus had, before the Jewish court—the representatives of God's chosen people Israel—witnessed a good confession regarding Himself as the Messiah, the Son of God, so now before Pontius Pilate—the representative of Gentile authority—He witnessed equally clearly and unequivocally that He was a king—though going on to explain that He was no rival to the Roman Emperor, no insurrectionist; for His Kingdom was not of this world (John 18: 36). Thus before Jew and Gentile; before the Sanhedrin and the viceroy of Cæsar; before religious and secular authorities, Jesus bore twofold testimony, as Messiah of Israel and King of kings.

During the trial before Pilate, however, there occurred the strange interlude of His being sent to Herod, in a vain attempt by Pilate to evade the distasteful rôle of executioner for the Sanhedrin. Herod Antipas, tetrarch of Galilee, and son of Herod the Great, was one of the Idumaean rulers set upon a puppet throne in Israel by the Romans. He might be regarded as occupying a half-way position between Jews and Gentiles; a man steeped in Jewish lore and traditions, though despised and hated by the people he ruled. He had at one time come somewhat under the spell of John the Baptist, and had an awed regard for that stern preacher: but lusts of the flesh had proved stronger than respect for the truth, and in order to please his incestuous wife he had put John in prison, and finally had beheaded him at the behest of her daughter Salome. Herod, haunted by superstitious fears that Jesus might be John the Baptist come to life again, had desired to see the One about whom he had heard such remarkable reports of miracles and mighty deeds. To him, however, Jesus would speak no word at all. He had nothing to say—as He still has nothing to say—to a man who had silenced the voice which testified against his sins.

Pilate yielded to the subtle threats of the Jews, and gave

sentence against Jesus; and therein he judged—not the Nazarene, as he thought—but himself; for by his own words he stands condemned for all time and for eternity, the coward who under pressure of threats violated every principle of justice, and gave up a man whom he had repeatedly pronounced innocent, to scourging and to crucifixion. In vain did he, in puerile dramatic gesture, endeavour to wash his hands of the guilt of that foul deed: not so can men absolve themselves from their acts, albeit committed against their own inclination and desires. What men do, they *do*, no matter what they may think or say; and ultimately, by their deeds they will be known and judged. Thus in the presence of Jesus, Pilate was fully revealed, in his weakness and vacillation, his readiness to subvert justice for his own interests, his signing of the death warrant of one whom he had declared to be not guilty. For fear of the frown of Tiberius, Pilate sent the Son of God to the gallows, and must answer for the most shameful violation of the judicial office ever perpetrated.

Jewish and Gentile judges thus judged themselves in passing sentence on Jesus. Nor was His condemnation the decision and deed of a few sinister men unrepresentative of their fellows: the people clamoured for His death, crying "Crucify Him," and deliberately called upon themselves the consequences of their deed—"His blood be on us, and on our children" (Matt. 27: 25). Romans matched them in callous and heartless malevolence against Him, putting a crown of thorns on His brow, mocking and smiting Him (vv. 27–31). All ranks of society, all types of people, thus united in rejecting and scorning and despitefully using the Lord Jesus. And all men still, of all races, cultures, ranks and creeds, faced with the challenge of Christ, pass some judgment upon Him—and in doing so, determine their own destiny. For, as Pilate discovered, there can be no evasion of the issue: ultimately all must decide, "What shall I do then with Jesus?" To submit to His claims as Messiah and King is to receive His grace as Saviour and Lord; to reject, is to place oneself at the bar of His judgment seat.

On His way to the cross to which Pilate condemned Him, Jesus paused to speak to some compassionate women who "bewailed and lamented Him" (Luke 23: 27–31). "Weep not for me, daughters of Jerusalem," He said, "but weep for yourselves . . ." and He went on to warn them of the doom awaiting Jerusalem, of which He had spoken to the apostles on the Mount of Olives only a day or two previously. In rejecting their Messiah, the people of Jerusalem had turned their backs upon the divine mercy, and exposed themselves to judgment and wrath. Swiftly the consequence of their sin and folly fell upon them, and their city was utterly destroyed. Their guilt was none the less because, in the will and counsel of God, the cross on Calvary effected His eternal purpose for the redemption of mankind. "Weep not for me," said Jesus; He was not a tragic casualty of the Jewish rulers' hate and Rome's oppressive might: He was going His appointed way as the Lamb of God: He was walking the road to the cross of His own deliberate will, and for His own appointed and gracious ends. "Weep not for me, *but for yourselves* . . ." Yes, and for all whose guilt is not cancelled out by that cross. For Jew and Gentile joined hands in sending Him there; the sin of all mankind nailed Him to the tree. And under its shadow every life is revealed, the destiny of every living soul is determined. Looking to that central cross on the hill outside the city wall, we hear therefrom words of pardoning grace and of life eternal —if we look in faith and hope and love; or we hear condemnation, if we reject its mercy and are heedless of its message. In the last analysis, *we* are the judges of Jesus; only to find that in judging Him we judge ourselves—and then, in that moment of revelation, to discover further that, in the paradox of the eternal orderings, the rôles are reversed: He is the judge, and His the judgment we were foolish and vain enough to think that *we* were pronouncing.

18

Arrival at Golgotha

THE Roman legionaries who nailed Jesus of Nazareth to His cross, did not for a moment think that this was in any way different from the many other crucifixions they had doubtless carried out. How could they know that this—to them —everyday event was the focus of all history; and that they were the cynosure of all eyes until the end of time? We regard the cross through the haze of twenty centuries of Christian devotion, which casts around it an aura of celestial beauty. In fact, of course, the cross was stark and terrible; and the experience of the One who died upon it, agonising beyond all description. We do not propose to dwell upon the physical aspect of His sufferings, however; but we would reverently take our place, in spirit, among the little group of those who loved Him so dearly as to stand at the foot of that cross, despite their terror.

Jesus had steadfastly proceeded toward this hour, this cross, knowing precisely what it would mean. This was no tactical triumph for His enemies; no disaster to His cause and Kingdom. Jesus was not caught up in a current of events from which He could not escape: this was no tragedy which overtook and overwhelmed Him. This cruel, ugly cross was the deliberate goal of His whole earthly life; the purpose for which He had come to this earthly scene. It was, as Peter declared on the day of Pentecost, according to the determinate counsel and foreknowledge of God.

The Lord had left His throne and kingly crown in order to die on this cross; He had plainly declared that He would give His life a ransom for many (Matt. 20: 28). This cross was an altar: the one altar of efficacious sacrifice for ever; and He was the one true availing sin-offering for all mankind. Thus He died, the Just for the unjust, to bring us to God; the Lamb of God, bearing away the sins of the world.

Bearing shame and scoffing rude,
In my place condemned He stood;
Sealed my pardon with His blood:
Hallelujah! What a Saviour.

This supreme manifestation of the love of God for rebellious man evoked—most terrible fruit of the fall—a display of the vilest and basest sins and passions and bestialities of which human nature is capable. We have considered something of the calculating evil of ambitious and hypocritical men: but, worse still, the outburst of unreasoning hostility toward One who had done nothing but good, in the cry of "Crucify Him!" was followed by the depraved taunting of the Sufferer as He hung in excruciating pain upon the cross. We all recognise the ugly trait in human make-up which takes morbid pleasure in the sufferings of others: but crucifixion was so terrible a manner of death that one would expect the most degraded and hardened person to be subdued to sympathy in its presence.

The Roman soldiers, whose trade was fighting and death, not unnaturally regarded this execution of a troublesome Jew as just another distasteful duty, which had as compensation the "perks" of His clothing—for which they gambled unfeelingly while they waited for Him to die. But that compatriots of the Sufferer could jibe and jeer at Him; that even the heartless men who had brought about His death could sink so low as to deride Him, glorying in their seeming triumph and unmoved by the least spark of human compassion—this was an exposure of human iniquity, the blackness and hardness and insensate evil of the heart, for which only the blood shed upon that cross could atone. Here was displayed the need for such a Saviour: the depravity which no other means could mitigate. Sin in its true nature as evil and transgression and iniquity was exposed at the cross. It was *sin*, not Roman nails, which fastened Him to the tree.

As our sin-bearer, Jesus hung there in awful solitude. Only one could "pay the price of sin," and as our representative and substitute He suffered the terrible isolation of the death of the cross.

None other Lamb, none other Name,
None other hope in earth or sky or sea;

None other hiding-place from guilt and shame:
None beside Thee.

Yet, in the paradox of both fact and faith, in His loneliness He was not alone; for on either side hung a malefactor, crucified for his misdeeds; and at the foot of His cross stood a few who loved Him and suffered in spirit with Him. The two thieves joined together at first in railing upon Him: tormented by their sufferings, and incited by the revilings of the mob, they spat out oaths against Him with their gasping breath (Matt. 27: 44). But after a while a remarkable change came over one of them. He became silent; and then he rebuked his companion in crime, in never-to-be-forgotten words: "Dost thou not fear God, seeing that thou art in the same condemnation? And we indeed justly; for we receive the due reward of our deeds: but this man hath done nothing amiss." Then turning his eyes to Jesus, he uttered the words which have inspired faith and hope in countless thousands of hearts, through all succeeding centuries: "Lord, remember me when Thou comest into Thy Kingdom" (Luke 23: 39–42).

Somehow, amid the torments of crucifixion this penitent thief had realised the difference between himself and his companion, and this other Sufferer. Did he remember stories he had heard concerning Jesus: indeed, had he been among the crowds listening to His parables and witnessing His miracles? We cannot tell: we only know that saving faith was kindled within his heart, and that on the very brink of death he heard the gracious, life-giving words which brought peace and joy past all understanding—even amid the agonies of crucifixion: words which have inspired faith and courage in myriads of others also, from that day to this.

In that moment the dying thief received the gift of eternal life, through trust in the One who hung, despised and rejected, on that central cross. For Jesus, in the act of dying, opened the gate of Paradise to a man who acknowledged that he deserved the penalty he was enduring, but cast himself on the divine mercy. And that penitent thief received the word of pardoning grace from One who, also suffering unto death, was nevertheless the Lord of life and the Prince of glory. On that very cross, Jesus displayed its power to save; He secured the first trophy of His redeeming grace, under the new covenant.

Three crosses stood on Calvary's brow, with Jesus in the centre. There, in the midst of that little group, He symbolised His position among all men, of all races and climes, and of all generations. He is in the midst of men, the One who suffered on their behalf, and is able to save unto the uttermost all who come unto God by Him. Equally He is the divider among men: for while on one hand are those whose sins are forgiven and who are saved by His grace, on the other are the unrepentant and unsaved, who go their chosen way into outer darkness.

The cross of Jesus is for all mankind the cross-roads where eternal destiny is decided. It is the one place of pardon and redemption; the one place where sin is judged and put away; the one place where fallen men can be born from above and become sons of God, heirs of life eternal. It is also the place where those who reject its mercy will receive everlasting condemnation.

Not all who watched Jesus on the cross were unmoved with compassion, for there was that little group, mostly of women, loving and loyal unto death. For them, the anguish of beholding Him upon the cross was almost equal to that of enduring the agonies of crucifixion: for to see a loved one suffer can be harder to bear than the suffering itself. Yet afterwards, they would count it the supreme privilege of their discipleship to have stood, in compassionate fellowship with Him, at the foot of His cross.

Without doubt their presence was a comfort to Jesus. He who had longed for the understanding and true companionship of His chosen friends on the road to the cross, and increasingly so as He drew steadily nearer to it, now derived strength and inexpressible consolation, we cannot doubt, from the loving solicitude of these devoted disciples who stood by Him in this dread hour of His direst need.

To them He addressed one of the seven "words" from the cross, revealing His tender thought and provision for the mother who had borne and reared Him, and whose heart was now pierced with that sword foretold by Simeon in the temple at His dedication three decades ago. Somehow her faith had faltered, and she had endeavoured to restrain Jesus in His ministry; but her love never wavered, and now she experienced the bitter sorrow which only a stricken mother can know. From that cross, however, she heard a word of filial tenderness and thoughtful concern, which was truly as balm in Gilead. With that word a new relationship was formed, symbolic of the new relationship He was initiating among His disciples, the "household of faith," the family of the redeemed. Here was a first-fruit of the cross, borne even while He hung and suffered there. From it have flowed all the ministries of healing and compassion in the Name of Christ, unto this day.

There followed three hours of portentous darkness, as if the very heavens were wrathful at what was being wrought against God's beloved Son: and then, as the more terrible darkness of dereliction enveloped the soul of the sin-bearer, from whom His Father turned away His face, there was wrung from His agonised spirit the most awful cry ever uttered in human speech: "*Eloi, eloi, lama sabachthani?*" We, whose sins have been atoned, can never have any conception of what it meant to Jesus, the sinless One, to be *made sin* for us: the utter horror of bearing substitutionally the sin and transgression and evil of all mankind—*becoming sin*, and being utterly alone, forsaken by God. That was the gall and the wormwood of the cross; that was the indescribable dereliction; that was the unutterable darkness of Calvary.

In that darkness Jesus tasted death in all its bitterness and terrible sting. In that dereliction He paid the price of sin—the sin of all mankind: mine and yours. Then, His spiritual agony having brought Him to physical extremity, He uttered the cry, "I thirst"—the only cry of human suffering wrung from His lips.

We have not dwelt upon the physical aspects of His Passion; but we do well to observe that He was not spared any of the horrors of the cross. In His true humanity, Jesus experienced no immunity from the full agonies of crucifixion. We began our studies with a reminder that this was the ultimate torture and indignity which Rome could impose upon despised and subject people. In full awareness of all its terrors, Jesus had steadfastly pursued His road to this cross; and now He hung and suffered there. Thus was He, as foretold of old, despised and rejected; a man of sorrows, and acquainted—oh, so poignantly—with grief.

His swollen tongue and burning throat moistened by the

vinegar given in response to His cry, Jesus summoned his fast-waning strength to exclaim, triumphantly, "Finished!" Love's redeeming work was done; the sacrifice for sin had been offered; atonement was made. Then, the final act of faith and filial submission: "Father, into Thy hands I commit my spirit." Thus Jesus died: by His own act and volition He laid down His life, a ransom for many. On that shameful yet glorious cross He took the very last step by which He fully accomplished that purpose predetermined before all ages. Thus He fulfilled the Father's will, and redeemed sinful men. He drank to the last bitter dregs the cup of suffering as our Saviour. He *died* . . . the Just for the unjust, to bring us to God.

Equally true is it that He was *put to death* by sinful men. Guilty mankind cannot escape the responsibility for that dread deed. Those who actually accomplished it were acting on our behalf—in the stead of all mankind—even as He died for all: it was the sin of the race which took Him to the cross and nailed Him there. "*Ye* . . . by wicked hands have crucified and slain," said Peter—not only to the crowd gathered in Jerusalem on the day of Pentecost, but to us all.

He died for all mankind: yes, but that fact would not bring the deep comfort and assurance my guilty heart needs, unless I can go further and say, with the apostle, "The Son of God loved *me*, and gave Himself for *me*." And that He did. It was my sin that took Him to Golgotha; it was for love of me—irrespective of all else—that He walked that road to the cross . . . from eternal ages; from the throne of His glory; from the manger, and from His baptism in Jordan . . . right to that central tree on Calvary. He took my place of judgment and death; He bore my sin and paid my penalty; He secured my pardon, and opened for me the gate of Paradise. That is the personal aspect of the cross, for every believer.

What shall we say, then, as we stand there at the foot of the cross? It is not enough to sing vaguely, emotionally—

> Love so amazing, so divine,
> Demands my soul, my life, my all . . .

From the loneliness of that tree the Lord Jesus invites us to follow Him in the way of the cross; into a companionship with

Him in His sufferings, and a conformity to His death. He asks us to go with Him outside the camp, bearing His reproach. He asks this because, for us as for Him, the cross is the gateway to the glory which follows. Through such fellowship with Him in death alone can we know the power of His resurrection, and find the fullness of life. It is the way the Master went: should not the servant tread it still?

19

And the Glory that Followed

THE road which led to the cross did not end there, or we should not be considering it now. Books which dwell upon the events of the dread day when Jesus died, and conclude at the tomb of Joseph of Arimathæa, concentrate upon only half of the Gospel story. Wondrously true it is that, as we each can say, with St. Paul, "The Son of God loved me, and gave Himself for me"—gave Himself up to the shame and agony of the death of the cross. But to become our Saviour He needs must not only be "delivered for our offences" but also be "raised again for our justification." It was not possible that He should be holden of death. Jesus of Nazareth was the Prince and Author of life; the Resurrection and the Life; the Living One, who submitted to death that, in dying, He might open the gate of eternal life for those who were doomed to die. By eternal decree, Easter day must follow Good Friday as morning follows night.

Of the fact of the resurrection there can be no reasonable doubt. It has been well described as one of the best-attested events of history. The evidence is overwhelming. And the suggestion sometimes made that Jesus had not actually died, but merely swooned upon the cross, and revived in the tomb, has never been regarded seriously. Rome attested the fact of His death. I used to wonder why crucifixion, with all its horrors, was the specifically fore-ordained mode of death for the Suffering Servant. If it was needful for Him to die, surely a less agonising manner of dying would suffice to accomplish the redemption of mankind. But in the wisdom of God, crucifixion was the appointed mode of His death, for a number of reasons. Among them was this consideration, that it would stifle for ever silly notions that somehow He had survived. Rome was thorough in all its operations; and no one crucified on a Roman cross ever survived. The soldiers of Imperial Rome certified the death of Jesus.

Most wondrous story ever told among men is that of the triumphant resurrection of the crucified Nazarene. Most thrilling note in the pæan of praise of the redeemed, is ascribed to the living Lord and ascended Saviour. For in His triumph over sin and death and hell, Jesus is the Head of the new creation, the Giver of eternal life to all who trust in Him, the great High Priest of the people of God.

Jesus had foretold His resurrection. Clearly and explicitly, He had spoken to His disciples concerning it, as He had sought to prepare them for the shock and sorrow of His dying upon a cross (Matt. 16: 21; 17: 22; 20: 17). He knew that He was to be crucified: He knew as surely that He would rise again on the third day. He had come in order to die; He was about to submit to death, in order that He might rise triumphant over it. Death was the essential gateway through which He must pass to His glory—that is, His glorification as Man, as Redeemer, as the Firstfruits of them that slept.

He went willingly to death because, in dying, He would rob death of its sting and deprive it of its tyranny. In dying He would take from death its terror, and transmute the tomb into the very threshold of life everlasting: the ante-chamber of His Father's abode. For the joy that was set before Him—the joy of "bringing many sons into glory"—Jesus endured the cross, despising the shame. He knew that the road to the cross led also to the glory that should follow.

In the Easter tidings many notes mingle: notes which strike the deepest chords in our human make-up, and answer to our highest aspirations and direst needs. There is ineffable tenderness in the greeting of the risen Lord to the weeping woman who loved Him devotedly; there is manly forthrightness in His restoration of the conscience-stricken Peter; there is stimulating reasoning with the disconsolate two on the road to Emmaus; there is irrefutable evidence for the wondering group in the upper room; there is kindly yet stern rebuke for the wilful doubts of Thomas; and stirring challenge for all His followers, to proclaim the glad tidings unto the ends of the earth.

It is characteristic of our human self-centredness that, even in considering the glorious resurrection of our Saviour, we think primarily, if not exclusively, of the significance of Easter-tide *for us*: the peace and joy it brings us, in the knowledge that our sins have been atoned, and our eternal felicity secured. Our Lord's resurrection as the guarantee of ours, is our chief concern. How seldom do we think of what the triumph of the first Easter day meant to the risen Lord Himself!

Thus, as we read of His first appearance, to Mary Magdalene, we conjure up in our mind's eye the scene outside the tomb, with the weeping woman asking the One whom she mistook to be the gardener, "Where have you laid Him?" and then, in a moment our hearts are athrill as we witness her sorrow turned into rapturous joy when He uttered her name, and she recognised those tender accents, and exclaimed in startled amazement, "Rabboni!" Yes, it is a wondrous, moving story indeed: and it enshrines great truths concerning the transformations which His resurrection has effected for us—banishing our despair, like hers, and heralding the dawn of celestial day.

But much—inexpressibly much—as His resurrection meant to Mary, what is that in comparison with *His* joy in accomplishing the purpose for which He came? He was still the Man Christ Jesus—the very same Jesus, bearing the marks of the nails which had pierced His hands and feet, and of the thorns which had crowned His brow, albeit He was no longer confined by the limitations of our human flesh; and if Mary rejoiced to hear her name pronounced by those lips which had been silenced in death and now spoke again with triumphant authority and divine grace, how must *He* have rejoiced to utter that transforming word! *His* sorrow, too, had been turned into joy—that joy for which He had endured the cross, despising the shame.

The utterance of that one word, "Mary," was the first proclamation of the Gospel message—for the very essence of the Evangel is the tidings of the resurrection, His and ours. It presaged the joy of the redeemed of all nations, in all ages until His Return in glory, when He shall present unto Himself His Bride, resplendent in the robe of His imputed righteousness: the Church gathered out from all the peoples of the earth. And the joy of the redeemed is an experience they share in fellowship with their Lord: it is an echo and reciprocation of *His* joy, into which He entered on that first Easter day.

A few hours after that meeting with Mary—having restored Peter to apostleship in an unrecorded interview, and having had also an ever-memorable walk and talk with two obscure disciples on the road to Emmaus, opening to them the Scriptures and asking, "Ought not Christ to have suffered these things, *and to enter into His glory?*"—He appeared suddenly in the midst of the assembled group of disciples in the upper room, although the door was shut for fear of the Jews. Again, we are accustomed to think of what that hour of revelation and restored faith meant to that band of distraught men, rather than the joy it afforded Him to banish their doubts and transform them into apostles of the Lamb and pillars of His Church. If the disciples were "glad when they saw the Lord"—as John records, with remarkable restraint—how glad was He to see the light of true understanding dawn in their eyes, hitherto darkened by their prejudices and preconceived notions; and to discern a true dedication to His Person and cause and will, which nothing could henceforward intimidate or quench. They would, indeed, from this time onward, follow Him whithersoever He might lead—even unto a cross, if need be: counting it now their highest privilege, whereas it had been their most terrifying fear.

Long years before, Isaiah had foreseen the day of Christ, and had foretold His going like a lamb to the slaughter. Perplexing as such a vision might be, the seer knew also that through the suffering of death He would achieve His purpose of grace: "He shall see of the travail of His soul, *and shall be satisfied.*" That is the Easter tidings. That is the triumph of the cross. The yearning of the Father-heart of God for fellowship with a people of His own image and likeness, rendering to Him responding love and willing devotion, is realised through Christ. In His resurrection and ascension He is the Federal Head of the new creation, Redeemer of His people, and Bridegroom of His Church.

Unworthy as we are, it is amazingly true that "His delights are with the sons of men." From among a rebellious race He is gathering unto Himself, through the merits of His death and resurrection, His Church: His Body, His Bride—His beloved in whom He delights. The Easter message comprehends not only His rising from the tomb, but also His ascension to the throne on high, His heavenly session and promised return, when His purposes of grace will be consummated in the completion of the Church and the marriage of the Lamb. That is the full range of the glory that follows . . .

That, also, is the joy which made Him esteem the walking of the road to the cross worth while. It is humbling to the dust to realise that He *thus* set His love upon us, unworthy rebels and defiled as we were, from eternal ages; for our sakes He was fore-ordained the Lamb of God; for us men and our salvation He was born in Bethlehem and endured the rejection and scorn and spitting, and the death of the cross.

> Were the whole realm of nature mine,
> That were an offering far too small . . .

But the whole realm of nature is not ours to give; nor does He require it. What He does desire is the love of our hearts, the devotion of all our ransomed being, such as will indeed satisfy His desire for fellowship and willing adoration. There is one way, supremely, of rendering this: it is by response to His call to keep Him company in the way of the cross. In so doing we shall ensure also our own highest good: for "if so be that we suffer with Him, that we may be glorified together"—and the context makes clear that "suffer" here means to be identified with Him in death and burial and resurrection (Rom. 8: 17, cf. vv. 10–16). He would have us to say, with Paul, "I am crucified with Christ: nevertheless I live; yet not I, but Christ liveth in me." When that is true, He sees of the travail of His soul and is satisfied. It is our privilege to contribute to that joy for which He endured the cross. *That* is the Easter tidings.

20

Our Identification with Christ

I N our survey of the road along which Jesus journeyed to the cross, we have repeatedly suggested that, as His disciples, we are invited not merely to meditate upon His steadfast purpose in preceeding thither, but also to walk with Him along that road. How, then, can we do this, two thousand years after that Roman cross was erected on Golgotha? It is not enough to re-echo the words of St. Paul, "I am crucified with Christ: nevertheless I live; yet not I, but Christ liveth in me" (Gal. 2: 20); we needs must interpret this apostolic declaration in the practical terms of everyday life in this twentieth century.

On the cross Christ bore our sins and died in our stead. In the reckoning of God our sin was judged and dealt with there, once and for ever. Through faith in Christ as our Saviour, we are identified with Him in that act whereby the divine judgment upon sin was effected and the divine wrath assuaged. We died in Christ; henceforth the High and Holy One regards us as dead unto sin and alive unto God: identified with Christ in death and burial and resurrection. So we can go on to say, with the apostle, "The life which I now live in the flesh I live by the faith of the Son of God, who loved me, and gave Himself for me." For the cross of Calvary is not only the means of ending our sinful and condemned life; it is also the beginning of the new life—the life more abundant which our Lord promised to His disciples. "If any man be in Christ," St. Paul declares, "he is a new creation . . ." or, as J. B. Phillips renders it, "For if a man is in Christ he becomes a new person altogether—the past is finished and gone, everything has become fresh and new" (2 Cor. 5: 17); and again, "we are buried with Him . . . into death; that like as Christ was raised up from the dead by the glory of the Father, even so we also should walk in newness of life" (Rom. 6: 4). D. W. Whittle, an American hymn-writer, expresses this thought in his well-known lines—

> Dying with Jesus by death reckoned mine,
> Living with Jesus a new life divine . . .

That is our position and state in the sight of God: identified with Christ in the historic act which had been so long foreshadowed and foretold, and was accomplished on Calvary; and in consequence "new creatures" in Him. This "great transaction," as Philip Doddridge described it, took place in the experience of regeneration; in the moment of new birth through faith in the Lord Jesus Christ as Saviour—be that "moment" a realised, decisive act of believing on Him and committal to Him, or a gradual process of response to the gentle constraints of His Spirit. However it happened, the child of God can joyously exclaim, "I am my Lord's, and He is mine." Our sins are blotted out; our hearts and lives are cleansed in His precious blood; we are redeemed, regenerate, born from above —and consequently we "walk in newness of life."

The principle of this new life, the Scriptures emphasise from beginning to end, is *faith*. As for the Lord, so for us: the decisive acceptance of the cross—in the act of submission to Him —must be wrought out by faith, in a continual realisation of that identification with Him in death and in His resurrection. Our earnest desire is that of the apostle, "That I may know Him, and the power of His resurrection, and the fellowship of His sufferings, being made conformable unto His death" (Phil. 3: 10).

We come closer, however, to the true significance of our Lord's words, "If any man will come after me, let him deny himself, and take up his cross daily . . ." when we realise their application to *self* as well as to sin. The veriest babe in Christ recognises that sin in the believer is an anomaly: we have died to sin, and should abide in that condition, by faith. Fewer Christians, alas, recognise as readily that *self* is an equally formidable enemy of our souls, and to it also we should die. This is brought out more forcibly in the *N.E.B.* rendering, "If anyone wishes to be a follower of mine, he must leave self behind; day after day he must take up his cross, and come with me." That is the deep note in the apostle's testimony in Galatians 2: 20, "I have been crucified with Christ: the life I now live is not my life, but the life which Christ lives in me . . ." (*N.E.B.*). The "I" is our most subtle, persistent adversary: we cannot subdue or sublimate it; our only way of deliverance and victory is through death to self, in identification with Christ. This nullifying of our sinful, self-centred life, and release into the glorious liberty of the sons of God, is essentially an activity of the Holy Spirit in us, as we affirm by faith our union with the Lord Jesus—and *manifest* that faith by reckoning ourselves to be dead indeed unto sin and alive unto God. We "deny ourselves" and take up our cross daily.

Our identification with Christ has therefore a double aspect: *judicially*, in His death on the cross two thousand years ago; and *experimentally*, in everyday life, continually, by faith. We *died* unto sin when Christ died; yet we are to *reckon ourselves dead* unto sin each moment of every day. Nor is this a mere passive attitude; we are to *mortify* our members—to put them to death; and to *yield* our bodies as instruments of righteousness unto God. We cannot do this of ourselves, and in our own strength: the whole secret of the Christian life is faith in the Lord Jesus Christ—experiencing the power of His resurrection as we abide in Him and walk with Him.

This leads us to the apostle's emphasis upon the fact that were are identified *with Christ*. Only so can we know the fellowship of His sufferings and be made conformable unto His death. In a true fellowship with Him of faith and devotion, we walk with the Lord in the way of the cross: we become His companions on that road—He keeping us company in our daily walk, as the apostles of old kept Him company in His walk steadfastly toward Jerusalem.

This denying—crucifying—of self is operative in the two spheres in which self finds its fullest expression and meets its fiercest temptations: the world, and the flesh. Christian people are too apt to regard "the world" as comprising certain aspects and activities of life of which they disapprove, and which they are quite ready to renounce. In so doing, they entirely miss the significance of New Testament teaching concerning *this present evil age*, from which the Christian is to be separated. Far more is included within that term than the pleasures and pursuits of "the world": it was the *spirit of the age* which our Lord condemned. Now we are all part and parcel of this our generation: but by the new birth we have been translated out of our natural habitat into the Kingdom of God. We are therefore strangers and pilgrims here, and should not be conformed to this age, but transformed through the renewing of our minds. This means far more than eschewing the fashions and indulgences of the world: it implies an essentially different spirit and outlook; a totally different attitude to the things and concerns of this life. We no longer seek supremely our own advantage and satisfaction, our career and well-being: we are no longer prisoners to such impulsions as "keeping up with the Joneses." We reckon ourselves dead to all such ideas and false standards; to the ambitions and passions of the world: rather, we recognise that we are not our own, but belong to Christ, and our paramount concern in the world is to fulfil His will and witness to His grace and power.

Similarly we have died in Christ to the *flesh*. Again, this is a term which Christians often misunderstand in their superficial designation of certain carnal sins as being "of the flesh." Now in the New Testament, the "flesh" is the totality of our personality in which *self* finds expression. Many pious people who eschew what they condemn as "sins of the flesh" are yet indulging the flesh in the more insidious and deadly sins of pride, self-opinion, self-esteem, censoriousness, covetousness, religious complacency—and many more. To these we should be dead, in our identification with Christ and denying of self —our walking with Him in the way of the cross.

Two cardinal factors in this grave matter call for emphasis. First, that we cannot crucify ourselves. The only way to die to sin and self, the world and the flesh, is to be crucified with Christ. That can be, in its practical realisation, through vital and living faith alone. It is a matter of personal response to the Lord Jesus Christ, and submission to Him in all His will for our lives. Yet in the paradox of the Gospel we have our part to play in the exercise of such faith: we are to mortify our members, to deny ourselves, to reckon ourselves dead. We must take up our cross daily and follow the Lord.

That leads to the second and supreme consideration: that

our identification with Christ is a reality in the measure of our true and continuing fellowship with Him. So often the bearing of the cross is regarded as merely the observance of a code of behaviour—denying ourselves certain things that we consider to be unfitting for a Christian; whereas it is essentially a matter of "walking with the Lord in the light of His Word." Jesus said, "If any man will *come after me* (i.e., keep me company), let him deny himself, and take up his cross daily, and *follow me.*" The cross is thus placed in the context of true discipleship. What a difference it would make in our attitude to the cross, if only we would grasp that, in our experience, it means vital union with Christ, abiding in Him, trusting and obeying Him, keeping Him company in the way—albeit along the road to Golgotha.

> It is the way the Master went:
> Should not the servant tread it still?

He is seeking to lead us, through our identification with Him in death and burial and resurrection, into the most intimate and abiding relationship with Himself; a relationship of true and deep faith and hope and love. This is our greatest privilege and joy this side of heaven. Its highest realisation is in the way of the cross.

As He steadfastly proceeded to the cross—from the very throne of glory—let us respond to His call to keep Him company in that way.

> "Take up thy cross," the Saviour said,
> "If thou wouldst my disciple be;
> Take up thy cross, with willing heart,
> And humbly follow after me."